GOD ALONE
SUFFICES

S. C. Biela

In the Arms of **Mary** FOUNDATION

COMMUNION OF LIFE WITH CHRIST THROUGH MARY

Fourth American Edition

Nihil Obstat   William C. Beckman, M.T.S.
                    Censor Librorum

Imprimatur   +Most Reverend Charles J. Chaput, O.F.M. Cap.
                    Archbishop of Denver
                    May 8, 2002

Published by
In the Arms of Mary Foundation
P.O. Box 271987
Fort Collins, CO 80527-1987
E-mail address: inquiry@IntheArmsofMary.org
Website: www.IntheArmsofMary.org

Translated by
Reverend Jaroslaw Zaniewski

Edited by
Anne Mary Hines   Joyce E. Pfaffinger
Michelle L. Curtis   Frederick M. Baedeker, Jr.

Cover, text design and artwork by
Ewa Krepsztul

"Decalogue for Faith Sharing" from Families of Nazareth Movement USA.
Used with permission.

In gratitude for the example of Our Blessed Mother, for whom God Alone Suffices.

Fourth American Edition
ISBN: 978-1-93-331462-4

CONTENTS

INTRODUCTION

O ne of the basic human psychological needs is the need for security, the feeling that we are in control, that we can manage the situation. From a human point of view it would be ideal if such a need were satisfied, however, then we would no longer need God. After all, are we not the ones who can manage just fine on our own? Are we not in control of our own lives? It seems certain, then, that we are the *masters* of our own destinies.

In Greek, 'Master' is *Kyrios*. *Kyrios* means the one who is in control of the situation (the Lord), the one who is like God. Such a person does not need God, because he or she is the one who holds the reins of events. It is in this context that we can discuss different kinds or different levels of reliance. To be in control is to rely on one's self.

In the realm of **material possessions** it means that we are the masters of our own standard of living, that we are reasonably secure. We have bank accounts, we have good jobs, and we have favorable prospects for financial advancement. On a material level we do not need God.

We can say that we only rely on ourselves, the "masters" of our own destinies, as if we were God. When we look at the many ways we approach different domains of the world, we notice a great number of idols. We can place our reliance on every pay raise we get and it can become a material idol for us. Every amount of money we save also becomes an idol because it increases the capital which is the basis of the trust we put in ourselves. Each of our newly acquired abilities also becomes an idol because it strengthens our faith and confidence in ourselves that there is no situation we cannot handle.

It is the same at the **psychological** level. We have a great need to control our feelings, emotions and other psychological reactions. We envision ourselves as a strong people who can manage in any circumstance, who hold on and who never lose control. It may also be the case that, rather than managing on our own, we would rather rely on other people. Another expression of our own greatness is the fact that we can always win our boss' favor, warm up to people easily, and gain allies and friends. We know how to follow the rules of socio-engineering. We arrange our relationships with others in such a manner that there is always somebody on whom we can count. Being a *Kyrios*, we ought to have our subjects and allies. We do so in order to reign freely and to make things go the way we want. Our children, our spouses, our friends and our acquaintances are – more or less – as we want them to be.

On material and psychological levels [respectively], we explain the problem of false reliances in two ways. One kind of reliance – our own *selves*, are the kind of *selves* that strengthen our confidence and help us deal with everything, which makes God completely unneeded. Alternately, the idols of our own *selves* can take the form of many idols. These can be the bosses, whose favor we have won, or any member of our interest groups, which we have manipulated in order to achieve our own goals. Our husbands, wives, or children are idols if they are – to our delight – living up to our expectations.

The situation is also the same on a **spiritual** level. When we have spiritual aspirations that draw us toward God, our selves become idols because we are confident about our own spiritual abilities. Even here we want to be in control because we think we know the way to God. We notice our own spiritual progress, so we become better people who are closer to perfection and thus we are happy with ourselves. Our *selves* are so wonderful that even God should find utter delight in us.

As on the other levels, here again we can see one idol, which is our own [individual] *selves* – managing our spiritual situation, being in control and feeling secure on the way to God. We have thought of everything. We have planned all the stages of our spiritual development and now we are calm and sure about achieving our goal. On the other hand we can see many idols. Every time we are satisfied with the good we notice in ourselves, every sign of our greatness, becomes an idol for us. Each time we make progress, each successful contact with God, becomes our idol. All real merits and achievements, good deeds and inner victories are sufficient to bring us peace and to assure us that we are in control of our own spiritual situations.

As described above, these are three expressions of the faith we have in ourselves on the three levels of our existence: the material, the psychological and the spiritual. We not only believe in ourselves at the present moment, but we also place our hope in ourselves for the future. If everything goes as it has been going up to now, we think we can manage in the future because the past and the present have assured us of our abilities. Of course it may be difficult, but so what? No work is easy. What is important is that our toil will be sweet because it will place us on the pedestal of the faith and hope we have in ourselves.

Above is a thumbnail sketch that portrays our old selves. It is a portrait of the structure and relationships we have with the world as described from the point of view of the Gospel. From the human point of view, our situation is really hopeless. Our selfish attitude causes us to rely on the basic need of the human psyche, which is the need to control everything. As such, we are determined to follow the path of human nature.

Divine revelation, however, proclaims God who mercifully watches the 'clownery' of our old selves, but who also – sooner or later – will want to show His love. This will lead us to the road to conversion. We will go through external and internal events that will crush the illusory image of successes that our old selves apparently achieved.

Through inner inspirations, through His continuous showering us with His uncountable graces, through emotional experiences or spiritual dryness, God will want to convince us existentially that we are not, and we cannot be, the masters of our own destinies. It is He who is the only *Kyrios*, the only Master. He will want to convince us that the faith and hope we have in ourselves are as illusory as any other fiction. They are going to fall apart and He is the one who will mercifully heal our wounds resulting from this process. He will try to convince us that He loves us more than life – that we are His adopted sons and daughters, who are created out of nothingness.

To the extent to which we are open to His grace, God will lead us to the deep water of truth. *Duc in altum* [put out into the deep water] – He will show us the ideal and will want us to convert to it because the ideal is the truth about us being children and about our utter poverty.

Maybe God will show us that there is no sense in our desires to please Him. Although God loves with a love of profound acceptance, the only thing He loves in this way is His own action in human souls. God only loves what He has created Himself, what His Divine action is and what is thus worthy of His delight. On the other hand, everything in human souls that does not belong to Him is also embraced by His love. It is the merciful love, the love of pity and forgiveness that wants to save and draw close to His merciful heart all that is little, unsuccessful and miserable.

Every situation that tempts us to be in control will bring about a polarization. If we are overwhelmed by anxiety, pressure, and stress, we may struggle unaided with the danger that threatens our own intensive desires. If the situation goes beyond our power, we may flee into illusions, deny the truth about the danger, and think to ourselves: "Everything is going to be all right," and so we busy ourselves with something else. But we can also choose the way of faith, trusting that the endangerment is the opportunity leading us to Jesus, who controls the situation, or, on the Marian way, to Christ through Mary. If it is she who is in control, then we only need to find shelter under her mantle and already we become calm and safe.

During her apparition in Guadalupe, Mary said to St. Juan Diego:

> My son, smallest of all, that it is nothing that frightened or afflicted you.
> Let not worry perturb your face, your heart...
>
> Am I not here, I who am your Mother? Are you not beneath my shadow and protection? Am I not the source of your happiness? Are you not in the hollow of my mantle, in the crossing of my arms?
>
> Do you need anything else?

Thanks to the enlightening action of grace we will be able to discover – so to say – two individuals in ourselves. The first, generated by the results of original sin, causes us to be the self-styled masters of our own destinies. On the other hand, our other selves will start to see a different reality – the reality that is implanted in us with difficulty by grace – the reality of being an evangelical child.

It is true that we are torn apart, as St. Paul says in his Letter to the Romans. We are torn in two and determined to engage ourselves in the battle between the two realities. The important thing to remember is that grace can win and the child in each of us can prevail. The child in each of us means somebody who lives in us according to the truth about our own clumsiness, nothingness and misery but, at the same time, expects to receive everything from the merciful hand of God.

Rev. Tadeusz Dajczer

Let nothing trouble you,
Let nothing scare you,
All is fleeting,
God alone is unchanging.
Patience
Everything obtains.
Who possesses God
Nothing wants.
God alone suffices.

ST. TERESA OF AVILA
Poesías 9

PART ONE

THE WORLD OF
ILLUSORY RELIANCES

> *The entire world is not worthy of a man's*
> *thought, for this belongs to God alone; any*
> *thought, therefore, not centered on God is*
> *stolen from Him.*

ST. JOHN OF THE CROSS
Maxims and Counsels

In what or in whom do I place my trust? On what or on whom do I count? These questions lead us to discover the problem of our false reliances. Seeking reliances[1] is what makes us function and live. It is truly the main engine of our endeavors. This tendency is so intense in us that we can call

---

[1] The expression "seeking reliances" is used here to express our relation to things or people. This relation involves – to a large or small degree – **counting on** a given thing or person and also seeking **sense** or particular **value** in them. This applies to the material, psychological and spiritual realms.

it the **'greed of reliances'**. We really cannot free ourselves from this tendency because when we lack reliances it leads to feelings of insecurity and fear and the anxiety of being threatened. On top of that, our need for security is one of the most intense human needs. As a result of this need, human beings intensely seek reliances in the realm of material possessions, placing their hope in different forms of riches, whether in the form of discrete objects, money, savings or success in the workplace. For many people, however, the psychological reliances that they find in other people are more important. We know this by the simple fact that we place a great deal of hope in other people, counting on them excessively.

Isn't what we seek and desire an illusion? Perhaps this activity of seeking and desiring reliances becomes just another mirage that endangers us because we then fall into the trap of feeling wounded and disappointed. At the same time, this hinders us from being united with God.

The human tendency to build illusory reliances is amazing. We really do not need much in order to create our own vision of the world, a vision that supposes to back up our plans and concepts. It seems as though we are incapable of existing without some illusory support. As people of weak faith, we cannot live without these illusions because we do not believe that God loves us with all our misery, and we cannot stand the truth either about ourselves or about the world that surrounds us.

IN THE SERVICE OF OUR OWN 'EGO'

Human beings – greedy because of our restless hearts – constantly want to seek support in things that seem measurable and concrete. In this way, we try to create a material system of security for ourselves. For this reason, we continuously look for acceptance, success and the expansion of our own abilities. Consequently, in desiring the approval for our own ego, we raise the ego on a pedestal and elevate it to the rank of an idol that demands praise and service.

ACHIEVEMENT ATTRIBUTED TO OURSELVES

Theoretically, we agree that everything depends on God. In day-to-day living, however, we often completely forget this. Only in the light of faith can we see that our reliances on money, material things, the economy, even our good health and our own capabilities become an illusion when we forget that they are meant for God. They are God's gifts that we ought to use according to the intentions of our Creator.

For example, **the money** that we earn by our work always **creates** a smaller or greater **illusion of security**. Because we think we can purchase everything that is needed for survival, therefore, it is easy to cultivate the conviction that the more we earn, the more secure we are in life. God, on the other hand, desires that we learn how to think in the category of faith. Based on our faith, sooner or later, God can question our sense of reliance, and this sense of our own self worth that is so connected to our job and the money that we earn.

We attribute our achievements at work to our own skills and competency. Have we ever thought that we owe all of our successes to our merciful God? Our Lord Jesus Christ, through His free gratuitous gift of grace, is the One who enables all of our achievements.

DIFFICULTIES THAT CAN BECOME OUR HELP

As long as everything goes according to our wishes, we continue to nourish the illusion about our own capabilities. God will begin to question our illusions. For example, in our work we may encounter a lack of success caused by our limited intellectual capability or by health problems. Then it may seem to us that everything at work is beginning to fall apart. However, the more a human support fails us, the more we are given the chance to think about the world differently by thinking in the category of faith. Such experiences are opportunities for us to forsake our sense of security in work and in the money we earn. When God undermines human abilities, He desires to show us that, without neglecting our efforts, we should most of all rely on Him.

Most importantly we should look at all these experiences in the light of faith, not as difficulties, but as **things that we should consider helpful** because they push us into the arms of Christ and enable us to turn to Him for help. Our Lord can then intervene and pour out His graces from which much benefit can result. Without these painful experiences these graces may never be received. Once our reliance is on God, the effect of our work is immeasurably better than if we toil and lean on the illusory sense of our own self-determination. We will then be convinced that this grace is given to us freely, as a miracle of God's mercy, and that it cannot be attributed to our own merit.

The less we rely on ourselves in our work, the more likely that God will intervene in our lives and use us to do whatever He desires.

FOR OUR OWN GLORY

Isn't it true that besides our own successes, we also consider our health and our good physical condition as something that we deserve and are entitled to possess, that we obviously should have these things as our own possessions? Therefore, we often forget that our good health is a gift from God and that this gift is only temporary. It is God Himself who gives us good health, and so we should receive His grace with thanksgiving and use it as a support. Our Creator gives us this grace for His greater honor and glory.

When we forget that our health is a gift, we simply waste all of our healthy years. Consequently, a huge part of our lives is wasted while we pursue our own will and live as though we are in charge of ourselves and, as if we are gods, are immortal.

One day, the moment will arrive when this grace connected to our physical health and well-being will come to an end. At that moment we might realize, with sorrow, that there were so many wasted opportunities for us to have fulfilled God's will and to have cooperated with His grace.

When taking care of our health, our talents or our material possessions, we are often convinced that we are going to use them to serve God. But in reality, unless our bond with Christ is very deep, we are only manipulating God by using them for our own honor. In reality, we seek our own glory. St. Albert Chmielowski[2] was very much aware of that danger when he gave up the earnings from his own paintings for the needs of his poor people. In this way he chose to work only for the glory of God.

God may make it impossible for us to use our money, capabilities or physical condition, even for so-called good goals, in order to prevent us from seeking our own glory,

---

[2] Brother (now a Saint, canonized in 1989) Albert Chmielowski (called by many St. Francis of Kraków) was one of the most promising young painters of Europe at the end of the nineteenth and beginning of the twentieth centuries. He regularly donated his earnings from the sale of his paintings for the needs of the poor people of Kraków. When he became aware of the danger of appropriating his talent as an artist, he decided to no longer count on the money from his paintings as a support for his poor people, and so he stopped painting altogether. It was not an easy decision, but he knew he had to do it. He then became a beggar on the streets of Kraków, and chose to work only for the glory of God and to count on the alms and offerings of people moved by the mercy of God. In this

which is normally tainted by our selfish interest. This may occur in our lives even though we are involved in His works.

SIMILAR TO THE RICH YOUNG MAN

Let us try to imagine that Jesus stands before us and utters the same words with which He approached the rich young man: "Go, sell what you have and give to [the] poor, and you will have treasure in heaven" (Mt 19:21). How are we to understand this call, having before our eyes the most important goal, which is our union with the Lord?

Sell everything and give to the poor – it seems that these words indicate quite clearly the call for one to abandon all material possessions for Jesus. Are we capable of doing this? And even if, in a heroic gesture, we are able to accomplish this, it is quite possible that by doing so we will build up our pride in a catastrophic way. Is it possible that a person can realize his own limitations and see his spiritual misery?[3] Can he accept this call of Jesus literally, and respond by giving up everything that, in itself, contains a type of material support? Certainly, this is not possible.

---

way, he focused on being one of the poor and loving them as they were, and bringing the love of God to them. Summary of the life of St. Albert Chmielowski is from an online forum: Jonathan Luxmoore, "Portrait of the Artist, a Holy Man." *Our Sunday Visitor* (October, 1997). http://www.catholic.net/RCC/Periodicals/OSV/971019.html.
[3] The meaning of the expression "spiritual misery" is introduced in the words of R. Garrigou-Lagrange: "Finally, while humility, which recognizes our indigence, should be found in all the just and should be in the innocent man, it is after we commit sin that we recognize practically not only our indigence, but our wretchedness: the baseness of our selfish, narrow hearts, of our inconstant wills, of our vacillating, whimsical, ungovernable characters; the wretched weakness of our minds, guilty of unpardonable forgetfulness and contradictions that they could and should avoid; the wretchedness of pride, of concupiscence, which leads to indifference to the glory of God and the salvation of souls. This

Persons, who are humble, know that they have to be saints. This requires them to give up everything while not building up their pride, which prevents them from following Jesus. So, instead of trying to give up all of our systems of reliance in a heroic way, it is better to say: *Lord, You know that I am a slave to the things which I possess.* "I am carnal, sold into slavery to sin" (Rom 7:14). *I am incapable of giving You anything, even the smallest things, because I am enslaved to them. But, You can do everything, so therefore I ask You to give me the grace necessary to follow You.*

ACCUMULATE OR LOSE

What is most important, then, is not our heroic action, but rather, our decision that is undertaken in the face of God's call. What are we striving for? Do we want to accumulate worldly reliances or do we want to lose them?

If we decide to follow Jesus, we have to replace the things that constitute our reliances with total support in the Lord. He does not demand that we give up everything right away, but He does want us **to agree to constant losing**. This can last for years, even until we die. If we do not want to lose, but instead we are focusing on accumulating reliances and on multiplying the things we possess – then we will have to depart from Jesus with sadness, just like the rich young man.

We cannot lose our reliances with just one act. The call to leave everything behind to follow Jesus consists of a

wretchedness is beneath nothingness itself since it is a disorder, and it occasionally plunges our souls into a contemptible state of abjection." R. Garrigou-Lagrange, "The Humility of Proficients," in *The Three Ages of the Interior Life* vol. 2 (Rockford, IL: TAN Books and Publishers, 1989), 121.

long journey toward holiness that can last many years; it becomes a **process** of constantly deepening our communion with Jesus. While it is important that we occasionally make the effort to give up something, even something significant, we must not fall into the illusion that we are capable of sacrificing everything for God. If we truly were full of love for Him, we would have sacrificed everything a long time ago. Our single acts of declaration, and even our concrete deeds – if they are not based on humility – give birth to pride. This pride distances us from living in communion with Jesus, which above all demands of us humility. If we do not love Jesus humbly, it is impossible to become poor, and our poverty becomes only an unrealistic abstraction.

We do not have to run toward sanctity faster than God intends. God, seeing how feeble and weak we are, will never allow us to undergo tests of faith that are too difficult for us. However, it is important to see in our poverty the opportunity to be filled with the richness of Jesus' love, and through our acceptance of losing, we can cooperate with the cleansing grace that God gives us. This tedious and lifelong process requires of us patience, endurance, and the virtue of longanimity.[4]

Our Lord Jesus Christ lives in communion with us to the degree in which we do not live in 'communion' with the false system of security offered to us by the spirit of this

---

[4] Longanimity from the Latin word *longanimus* means greatness of soul. It expresses much more than simple patience. It is lack of precipitateness. It entails understanding, toleration, capableness of forgiving, knowing to wait and to offer a new opportunity. Longanimity means **not to be discouraged for having to wait a long time for the fruits of our own efforts** and while facing difficulties of life, too.
  "In the Holy Bible longanimity is one of God's characteristics due to which God can condescend with His anger and punishment, granting to the sinner

world. This false system of security is always destructive and can ultimately lead to condemnation.

If, then, our Lord Jesus were to stand before us and utter the same words He uttered toward the rich young man, we would have to humbly admit to our enslavement. But, at the same time, we would have to joyfully agree to lose our various illusory reliances – to lose them through our communion with Jesus and reliance on His love.

a merciful term in order to give him the opportunity of conversion and penance. Therefore, longanimity is a divine attribute. In the New Testament longanimity is given to the 'new man' as a charism and a gift from the Holy Spirit." *Dicionário Enciclopédico Bíblico, 5ª Edição*, s.v. "longanimity." "In the Gospel God gives to mankind the example of longanimity in the parable of the unforgiving servant – Mt 18, 21-35." *Dictionnaire Encyclopédique de la Bible*, s.v. "longanimity."

Chapter 2

Where Your Treasure Is, There Will Your Heart Be

It is our lack of faith that results in our seeking reliances other than God. Subsequently, our treasure consists of false reliances, and this can be every thing, project, or idea to which we surrender our hearts.

THE CULT OF THE GOLDEN CALF

An idol can be anything that we allow to capture our hearts. We are capable of adoring many idols because, in actuality, many things can be a source of our reliance. For example, our home can be an idol that we take care of as if it were a loved one. It can be decorating our homes, our clothes, our car or our school. It can be any job that we hold in such high regard as to think it worthy enough to burn out over or to die for. Our Lord clearly said: "For where your treasure is, there also will your heart be" (Mt 6:21). These words describe precisely our relation to the things we possess. If a particular thing or idea absorbs our attention to the point to which it hinders God and His will, or if it becomes a reliance and a goal in itself, having connected it with our plans and dreams, then we really are surrendering our heart to this material thing that is only a some*thing* not a some*body*.

When the Israelites grew impatient for the return of Moses who was conversing with God on Mount Sinai, they made a statue out of gold to be their idol and they honored it (see Ex 32:4). By adoring the golden calf, they **put their hearts** in this dead thing, which was the invention of their hands.

Do similar 'cults' have a place in our lives too? Are there any ideas, tasks, or things that we are ready not only to live for, but also to die for?

HOW SHOULD THE THINGS OF THIS WORLD SERVE US?

Our Heavenly Father created the world in order that we use it for His greater glory. He desires that the things of this world serve us in our sanctification, and because of that we need to keep a proper distance from worldly things. We should avoid relying on worldly things and treating them as if they were personified. Instead, we need to treat them as mere instruments.

Consequently, we can take advantage of everything in a **worthy** way, in a good way that is **in accordance** with the intentions of God. Our home, our work, even our involvement in the things of the Church, and our noble plans and apostolic endeavors: all are simply **means** to our true end. They are means that God gives us to rely on Him and be more fully united with Him.

If our heart is with God and is uniting with His will, then those various means bring us closer to our union with Him. They are then being properly treated as objects. Otherwise, we may start treating objects as if they were persons and persons as if they were objects.

If our home or our work becomes such an enslaving reliance, then we will frequently treat people as mere instruments to help us achieve our desired goal. Such an attitude is in direct contradiction to the Gospel, which tells us that Christ died for every person and that every person is a temple of God worthy of our highest respect. Jesus said: "Whatever you did for one of these least brothers of mine, you did for me" (Mt 25:40).

GOD IS AGAINST IDOLATRY

How can we be united with our Lord if we serve mammon?[5] In this case, the container of our soul, which is filled to the brim with things and projects, cannot receive the Divine Guest. This would be similar to inviting someone to our room, barricading the door with numerous pieces of furniture and being amazed that the person does not come in.

---

[5] "Mammon: The New Testament Greek word *mamonas* occurs in Luke 16:9, 11, 13 and Matthew 6:24. This word was 'borrowed' from Aramaic and refers to material wealth and prosperity, especially property (Lk 16:9, 11). The word can be used to personify wealth (Mt 6:24, Lk 16:13) as a 'master' at enmity against God." *Catholic Encyclopedia* (1991), s.v. "mammon." "This personification, however,

Holy Scripture tells us that our God is a jealous God (see Ex 20:5; Jer 5:19). If we get emotionally involved in the things of this world, and if we seek reliance on them and let them become our idols, then we are guilty of idolatry. Consequently, our Lord, who is jealous of our human heart, will sooner or later oppose this condition. He may then decide to destroy our idol. We see an example of this in the Old Testament when, with the hand of Moses, He hit and destroyed the golden calf. Likewise, we may lose our home that has become an idol for us. Similarly we may lose anything that absorbs our heart. God may oppose our work or even our good deeds for the Church.

Our hearts are made for God and only for Him. Is it worth it to give our heart to anything that is only a 'means', that is, something that exists today and may be gone tomorrow? Isn't it a better idea to take advantage of these means for the greater glory of God in order to be more united with our Lord?

It is to our benefit to take care of everything with the utmost involvement that Jesus expects from us, while remembering that everything can be taken away from us tomorrow. And when this happens, we should leave behind everything, the way He wants us to, and not worry about it.

IN GOD'S VINEYARD

When we look at the world with the eyes of faith, we can perceive that it is God's big vineyard, and all of us are

is purely literary; there actually never was a pagan god or demon called 'Mammon', as is sometimes wrongly supposed." *New Catholic Encyclopedia* (1967), s.v. "mammon."

workers hired by God; from Him we receive our work and our worthy recompense.

In our work, then, we should take great care to make sure that it is pleasing to God, not to people, and that our work is connected to God's design for us. We have to carry out our work in accordance with the intention of the vineyard's Owner, and then this work can sanctify us and help us on our way to being more united with our Redeemer.

When we work in this way, trying to fulfill God's will, we may either receive the acceptance of those around us or be criticized for it and be met with misunderstanding. But even if we lose our job, it should not matter that much to us. After all, people do not give us employment, but rather God, who can take it away at any moment. Similarly, He can take away our life at any time. Our lack of work and our seeking after it without results can also contribute to our sanctity if we discover God's presence in this experience – God who holds everything in His hands.

Without seeking God's will, our work can internally destroy us and direct our attention toward 'having' at the expense of 'being' for Christ. And so, if much of our time is taken up by work and our salary is bigger than our needs, it is important that we ponder God's will. Perhaps God does not want us to be so involved in our work.

When we stand in truth before God, it is important to admit that we are often burdened with stress and fear because of our desire to gain another person's approval. By seeking reliance on our workplace, we place our hope in something that at anytime may cease to exist. Similarly, we can say that the entire world is passing away in accordance with revelation (see 1 Cor 7:31).

TO REST WITH THE LORD

Both our work and our leisure time are given to us so that we may deepen our bond with God and seek our support in Him. If we try to see God and to seek His will in everything that He bestows upon us, then our time for rest will strengthen our faith in God's omnipotent love.

When we spend time in front of the television, we very seldom think about God's presence connected to this gift. But isn't it God who has allowed the development of different types of instruments for our use, in spite of the fact that we frequently use them for the wrong reasons? He expects that even these gifts will allow us to discover His will. When we are at the movies, the theater, or in front of the television and we witness human sinfulness portrayed, it indicates that there is evil in the world. Isn't this the way in which God asks us to call upon His mercy for the world? After all, when He speaks to us through the media, He expects that we will awaken in ourselves a deeper, more reflective approach to the world around us.

Isn't it true that the way we spend our leisure time is quite often leading us astray and as a result, closing us to the will of God? Is it not God's will that we spend our free time in such a way that the spiritual and psychological needs of our loved ones can be met? The point is: our leisure time is an opportunity to find support in God and in His will for us at each moment.

Therefore, at work and at rest, in endeavors undertaken for the Church, and in every other moment of your life, there is only one thing that matters: **God and yourself**[6] – who chooses Him and desires to be united with Him. God bestows upon you all the things of this world that you may take advantage of them along the path to sanctification. In this way, you can undergo a transforming union with the One who loves you unconditionally.

---

[6] "Live as though only God and yourself were in this world so that your heart may not be detained by anything human." John of the Cross *Maxims and Counsels* (trans. Kieran Kavanaugh and Otilio Rodriguez in *The Collected Works of St. John of the Cross* [Washington, DC: ICS Publications, 1973]) 65.

CHAPTER 3

THE MIRAGE
OF PROSPERITY

Stubbornly, we seek the deceptive light of human love[7] that can lead us, not only toward people, but also toward things. Through these we try to become 'somebody' in our own eyes or in the eyes of others. During the purification of the dark night,[8] God will show us how illusory are all these human supports, either in the psychological or material realms. This process of unmasking our illusions is necessary. Without experiencing this truth about ourselves and genuinely admitting to it, we will continue living in this mirage and striving after human reliances, concentrating our efforts on 'having'. This, unfortunately, is always done at the expense of our 'being' and the goal of our being is, ultimately, Christ *being* in us.[9]

---

[7] Cf. St. Thérèse of Lisieux, *Story of a Soul*, trans. John Clarke (Washington, DC: ICS Publications, 1996), 83.
[8] St. John of the Cross *The Dark Night* (trans. Kieran Kavanaugh and Otilio Rodriguez in *The Collected Works of St. John of the Cross* [Washington, DC: ICS Publications, 1991]) 1.1.
[9] *The Redeemer of Man (Redemptor Hominis)* Encyclical Letter of Pope John Paul II, March 4, 1979, no.16, trans. "Vatican" (Boston, MA: Pauline Books and Media, 1979), 31-35.

HOW MUCH DO WE NEED?

To the degree in which God penetrates our lives more fully with His grace, we will see more clearly that, if we want to live according to the Gospel, we cannot really serve both God and mammon. Jesus said: "No servant can serve two masters. He will either hate one and love the other, or be devoted to one and despise the other. You cannot serve God and mammon" (Lk 16:13). It is important to add here that it is not only the person who takes advantage of his wealth in an egocentric way that lives for mammon, but also the one who desires to take advantage and have some type of control over his environment. This person, who **desires** prosperity and finds in it a sense of security, also lives for mammon.

The Israelites, who traveled through the desert to the Promised Land, did not lack anything that was necessary for their survival. They did not have to worry about tomorrow because God Himself was taking care of it. When God decided to put them to the test of hunger and thirst it was not His intention to destroy them. Those difficult experiences were meant to free the chosen people from idols and to teach them to rely on God alone.

Similar things happen in our lives. God does not want us to live in misery; rather, He wants to give us what we need. The problem lies in our judgment: what do we **really need**? There is much pretense involved in the realm of our material needs. We constantly redefine what constitutes a good standard of living. Desiring more and more to lean on material things, we simply increase our expectations. We willingly yield to this **hidden escalation of pretenses**.

For example, when exchanging our car for a better one, we take it for granted that possessing the newer model is good for us. If we already have a comfortable apartment, we consider it a natural progression to own a home, and later, a worthy endeavor to start building a bigger and better house. And when the time comes that God opposes our plans and disallows us from fulfilling our pretenses – whether through difficulties at work, health problems, or many other ways – we feel that we are being treated unfairly.

We fail to see, however, that our Heavenly Father removes from our lives only what can become an obstacle in the way to our salvation.[10] He loves us and knows better what we need.

If, while relying on God, we accept all the stripping with thanksgiving, discovering in it God's gifts, then gradually we will allow the words of Christ to be fulfilled in us when He says: "For my yoke is easy, and my burden light" (Mt 11:30).

ACCUMULATING SURPLUSES

When the Israelites were journeying through the desert to the Promised Land, God desired that they gather only the amount of manna they needed for one day. The ones who

---

[10] St. Teresa of Avila wrote the following hard words about greed as a great obstacle to salvation: "What is it we buy with this money we desire? Is it something valuable? Is it something lasting? Oh, why do we desire it? Miserable is the rest achieved that costs so dearly. **Frequently one obtains hell with money and buys everlasting fire and pain without end. Oh, if everyone would consider it unprofitable dirt,** how harmoniously would the world proceed, how many lawsuits would be avoided! What friendship there would be among all if there were

gathered more than they needed soon discovered that their surpluses decayed.

How do our savings serve us? It seems that they constitute an 'accumulation of manna,' becoming an illusory source of security that prevents us from relying on God and His will. If we allow our reliance on these surpluses to replace our faith in God – and such is our human nature – then we are living an illusion. In contrast, when we lack savings, we are forced to live from day to day, and by necessity, we have to rely more on God. The way in which we readily rely on surpluses reveals the feebleness and fragility of our faith. Such weak faith is unable to protect us from fears and anxiety about the future.

When we gradually begin to lose our illusory reliances, which up to this point have been the main source of our security, we will be convinced that there is no need for us to have so many surpluses. Then, to our amazement, we will discover that we become happier when we are poorer.[11]

That is why Jesus said: "Whoever loses his life for my sake will save it" (Lk 9:24). That is the correct perspective for holiness – to lose for Christ all of our reliances, to lose everything that we consider to have some value to us. Yet we become petrified at the simple thought that we would have

no self-interest about honor and money! I think this absence of self-interest would solve all problems." Teresa of Avila *The Book of Her Life*, vol. 1 (trans. Kieran Kavanaugh and Otilio Rodriguez in *The Collected Works of St. Teresa of Avila* [Washington DC: ICS Publications, 1987]) 20, 27. p. 183. Emphasis added by author.
[11] "We experience such great peace when we're totally poor, when we depend upon no one except God." Thérèse of Lisieux, *Her Last Conversations*, Aug. 6, no. 4, trans. John Clarke (Washington, DC: ICS Publications, 1977), 137.

to lower our standard of living and perhaps renounce even a very small portion of our possessions.

THE RICH MAN'S DIFFICULT ROAD TO THE KINGDOM

The person who wants to acknowledge his dependence on God in everything will have to agree to accept material poverty. Otherwise, this desire to be dependent on God will only be a theory.

What is the chance that our children will be able to live daily according to the Gospel if we ourselves do not give them a proper witness in our own lives? If we elevate our reliance on money, our high standard of living, or our comfortable lives to the rank of an idol, then our words will not have any value. Even in the matter of cultivating an interior life, our words will not have any significant impact on our children.

In addition, even if our spiritual maturity is such that we are able to be detached from rich things, a comfortable life style, and a well equipped house, who can guarantee that our children will also be detached from these things? Who can guarantee that they will not feel superior to those who are less fortunate?

The pressure of the environment pertaining to material reliance is so great that if parents do not give a believable testimony from their own lives, no amount of moralistic discussions will suffice to equip their children to withstand such pressure.

If, through our attitudes, we show them that money is more important than our supernatural lives, then our words about living according to the Gospel will be rejected by our children – if not before, then during the time of adolescence. It is important not to fall into the illusion that our children do not clearly see how we really live and what we truly rely upon.

After all, money is not given to us to feed our **pride of possession**, or for us to rely on it, or for it to enable us to lead a life of luxury. The money does not belong to us. It is given to us by God, who desires that we be wise in distributing and multiplying it – as biblical talents. Consequently, in the light of faith, we understand that God entrusted these talents into our hands not to necessarily double or triple our bank accounts, but rather to fulfill His plan. Sometimes, multiplying our talents may mean giving away everything we possess.

When we look at our family's material situation, we must always take into consideration the most important goal of our lives, that is, our sanctity and the sanctity of our children. If we think seriously about holiness, then money is equivalent to garbage. Money has value only to the degree that it serves us according to God's will.

Since this detachment to prosperity does not come easily, we must attempt to stand in the truth, admitting to our enslavement. Then, with humility, thank Jesus for loving us as we are and for desiring to be united with us.

Then, after some time, something will be born in us and we will bear witness to the conviction that this really is a truth. At that time Jesus will be able to be united with us to some degree. Consequently, everything can begin to change if Jesus Himself will look at the world and at people through us and in us. His holy Presence will free us for a moment from all worries. The serious problem of running away from ourselves and from God's presence in prayer will disappear because God Himself will become our concern for us and He will be the prayer within us. The problem of desiring security only in this world will disappear because God will become our only support.

CHAPTER 4

THE PROBLEM OF RELIANCE ON MARRIAGE

For couples, who enter the sacrament of marriage, the most important psychological reliance is usually their spouses. Even in the initial stages of dating, while looking for a spouse, consciously or subconsciously, people are looking for someone on whom to rely. Even though men and women have a different understanding of reliance, they both pursue it with like eagerness.

THE PERIOD OF FASCINATION AND LOSING ILLUSIONS

In a woman's relationships, it is important for her to have psychological support, and to have someone who will understand her, take care of her, and show her abundant kindness. The problem is that only God can respond to and fully satisfy this desire for love within a woman's heart. It is difficult, however, to grasp God and since our human nature demands something concrete, this desired ideal is sought after in the man she chooses to be her husband. Men behave differently, but, in their hearts there is also a deeply rooted desire to lean on somebody. They long to care for and receive care from their wives.

Couples are usually fascinated by one another during their initial period of engagement. Out of fear of turning the other person off, couples put their greatest effort into respecting and fulfilling each other's expectations and needs. This is motivated by egoism. This self-preoccupation cannot be avoided, even by people who have faith and who desire to put God above their own caprices.

This engagement period is a time dominated by mutual interest, mutual happiness of being together, and making beautiful plans for the future. This period of fascination usually lasts until sometime after the wedding. During this early period together, the couple continues to mutually adore each other and God gets pushed aside.

But after this initial period of living in illusion, which is based to a large degree on emotions and feelings, both husband and wife begin to see each other and their relationship in a truer light. Later they begin to recognize the things that previously they were blinded to, for example: their spouses' egocentric approach, egoism, pride, greed, etc.

This process of losing marital illusions is connected to suffering, but in our journey to sanctity, it is a very precious gift. The less that the spouses can rely on each other, the greater the chance that they will start to desire Christ, and in Him they will begin to discover the only true support.

MARITAL IDOLATRY

Each spouse ultimately has to fall in love with God as the only true source of love in his life. All aspects of a person's existence, including married life, lead to and prepare each spouse to espouse God.

Unfortunately, in marriage, there are husbands who treat their wives as idols, and thus fulfill all of their wives' whims. At the same time, wives can easily fall into the temptation of satisfying their husbands' egocentric expectations under the pretenses of married love. On each side there is enormous vanity. The admired spouse is in danger of self-contentment, while the other one, who is treating his or her spouse as an idol, in actuality, is despising Christ living in that person, and in a sense, is sinning against the first commandment.

Obviously, spouses should be kind toward each other. The temptation, however, to find substitute forms of happiness within the marital relationship is like poison, leading to abuse, deviation, and bitterness; it brings distaste and emptiness into a person's life. We are not able to be truly happy and to have meaning in our lives when we close ourselves off to God.

TRUE LOVE IN MARRIAGE

Loving our spouse does not require us to worship and adore him or her. Giving divine honor to that person would constitute idolatry, not love. To love our spouse, we need to discover Christ in him or her. We have to see the face of the

Redeemer in the features of our spouse, and at the same time, to fully accept the entire truth about our partner.

A person who seeks a true love tries to see the spouse in the light of faith and tries to view him or her the way that God does. Consequently, we should frequently try to seek the answer to this question: *How does God love my husband / my wife?* It is in this way that we should try to relate to our spouses.

True love in marriage can be practiced in various ways, but will not always be easy for the other person's ego to accept. It is important that we try to imitate God in our relationship with our spouse, even when doing so may cause some pain to the spouse. We can be sure that this pain will not hurt the spouse as we think it will.

WHAT TO DO FOR THE BURDEN TO BECOME LIGHT

It can become extremely difficult to adopt this posture of faith in our daily lives with our spouses. Quite often it will simply **be impossible** to look at our spouses through the eyes of God. However, we have to remember that what counts most of all is that we **attempt** to do this, not that we always succeed. We need to humbly turn to God and beg Him to grant us the grace of looking at our spouses as if through His eyes. We have to ask ourselves these questions: *Are we doing this? Are we asking God for such grace? Are we begging for Him to dwell in us, live in us and use us as instruments in His relationship to our spouses?*

What is very important here is the truth. Let us not be afraid to admit the truth before God that we are unable to love Him, our spouses, or even ourselves in a harmonious way. Admitting to this truth, together with the assurance that Jesus loves us as such, will help us to accept our own evil and the evil of our spouse. It will help us to look at our family more in the light of faith. Then it will become less painful for us when God strips us of the illusion that we can rely on our spouses instead of relying more completely upon God. God will show us that we cannot find reliance in another person, and in this way the 'marital yoke' will not be as bitter and the burden will not be as heavy – as is always the case when we will allow the yoke and burden to become Christ's.

If our marriage situation seems to be bitter and unbearable, it is often because we ourselves put the burdens on our shoulders, the yoke coming from our pride and close-mindedness to God's will. Jesus does not intend for us to take on this burden.

CHAPTER 5

FAMILY AS OUR RELIANCE

A lthough we know that our family in marriage should be our road to holiness, in practice we view our family purely through human eyes instead of looking at our family in the light of faith. In choosing the vocation of marriage, we are motivated simply by our desire to find reliance within the circle of our dear ones through the bonds of blood.

THE DESIRE OF FULFILLMENT

Usually, spouses see their desire to become parents as a natural way to fulfill their love. The marital relationship undergoes change, however, after the first child is born. The husband will have to discover and accept the fact that the newborn has special rights to the feelings of his wife.

A woman desires to have a baby as a part of herself. She hopes that this baby will make her life more meaningful, **filling up** the emptiness and loneliness within her. Very often the wife expects that the newborn will fulfill her and give her what she is unable to receive from her husband. At the beginning, those desires usually are 'fulfilled'. The child responds beautifully and completely to the mother's feelings, becoming tightly united with her. However, this egoistic expectation of fulfillment through her child does not constitute true love.

True love is realized when we are motivated to fulfill the true, most precious needs of another person, desiring to make this person truly and fully happy. It is not when we are motivated to make ourselves happy by helping the other person. Certainly, a mother desires to serve her child and make her child happy, but she usually expects **mutuality** from the child. She receives this mutuality when her child reciprocates her love with a smile, a certain look, and/or special gestures. This reciprocation is the biggest reward. However, it becomes very easy for the mother in this situation to begin leaning on the child as if leaning on an idol. It becomes very easy to forget that the only reliance we can find is in God, and besides Him, we cannot find anybody who will love us fully and truly to the end.

WE OFTEN SAY: "IT IS NOT THE WAY I WANTED IT TO BE"

To confirm this idea that parents want their children to be a source of reliance, the situation will arise when a child, for the first time, fails to reciprocate the parents' love. When the parents respond to this situation with disappointment, they discover that their parental hopes are merely illusory, and those hopes begin to fall apart like a house of cards before their very eyes. The shattering of this illusion brings pain and suffering to the parents connected to the realization that the child is not behaving according to their expectations.

We often have very concrete expectations, which we place on our young son or daughter. These expectations largely depend on our physical, psychological or spiritual development. It can be said that we do not accept in others, especially in our children, the things that we do not tolerate in ourselves; while, in contrast, we do accept the things that we are able to tolerate and understand in ourselves. When we desire for our child to exemplify our own expectations and dreams (especially the unfulfilled dreams of our own lives – our own vision of what it means to be a person), then we rely on a very subjective concept of education.

However, isn't true love connected to a desire to take care of a child in accordance with the **plan of the Maker rather than our own** desires? Earthly parents, in any case, have the simple task of fulfilling God's will in regard to **God's children**, who are merely entrusted to them here on Earth.

Nevertheless, in practice, this rule is frequently broken. Parents do not respect God's plan with regard to their children, but rather want the children to fulfill their own expectations and whims. And when the child does not fulfill them, the parents undergo various disappointments and setbacks in their own minds. Unfortunately, it follows that they force the child to adapt to their own dreams and desires. At this point, the parents forget the essence of true love: the child is not meant to complete them, but rather, they are meant to fulfill the child in accordance with God's plan.

THE REBELLIOUS STAGE OF ADOLESCENCE

When children enter adolescence, they begin seeking with greater intensity their own identities and their own ways of life. Then the first wave of rebelliousness sets in. When this occurs, this behavior should be read as a protest against the egocentric expectations of their parents who seek to fulfill themselves and to feed their own illusions through the accomplishments of their children. The more parents have relied on their child up to this point, the greater the child's rebelliousness will be.

All of these developments bring about a lot of unexpected tension and suffering, but this conflict also becomes a precious grace that cleanses the parent/child relationship. This time of rebelliousness should make the parents more aware of the fact that a child has the right to his or her own way, which the parents cannot possess.

If, as mothers and fathers, we really want to rely on God, then we will do whatever it takes to fulfill in our children what is important for them. We will want them always and everywhere to believe that God loves them forever and **unconditionally**, regardless whether they are successful in a particular field or experience repeated failures.

What is our reaction to the disappointments in the lives of our children? Our usual reaction is to not accept these disappointments, a response that arises from our inability to accept our own failures. Then unfortunately, when our children undergo failures, we neglect to provide the love for which they hunger and yearn.

Each person, after all, wants to be loved unconditionally, regardless of the fact that he commits evil and fails. Each one of us desires this unique, complete and true love that God shows us. When a youngster does not receive this love through his parents, he becomes rebellious and goes overboard in protesting against this insufficiency.

As long as parents rely on their son or daughter to fulfill their **own expectations, they paralyze the child**. The only rescue is to seek reliance on God, undertaking this battle in order to convince their child about the unconditional love of the Heavenly Father. Then the child will be able to learn how to get up after each fall, listen to the Creator, and enter into a dialogue with Him. When the teenager becomes convinced of the unconditional love of God, he will want to seek God's will and be obedient to Him.

RELIANCE ON GROWNUP CHILDREN AND ON GRANDCHILDREN

The tendency for parents to seek an illusory reliance on their children does not fade away, even when the children become grownups. This tendency manifests itself in the parents' desire to know all of the endeavors of their adult children. We fail to understand that, at this point in our children's lives, they are entitled to have a private, intimate relationship of their own with the Creator – the only Father.

When our children grow up and have children of their own, our reliance spreads further to encompass our grandchildren. New conflicts and sufferings arise because we forget that parents, not grandparents, are responsible for raising their children.

If we truly want our grandchildren to fall in love with God, for Him to become their only means of reliance, and His will to be their only food, then we will not count on our grandchildren fulfilling expectations in our lives. We will understand that we should focus on fighting for only one thing – that the grandchild will be fulfilled in a way that will lead him to what is most important – a relationship with our God, the Father.

The best thing for a child will be for us to lead him to falling in love with God, who is his only Father and Mother. How wonderful it would be if we led children to being in love with the will of the Creator, awakening this desire in the children, a desire similar to that of our Savior who lived on this earth and who said: "My food is to do the will of the one who sent me and to finish his work" (Jn 4:34). The goal is not that children fulfill the will of their earthly parents or grandparents, but rather, the will of the Heavenly Father.

If children desired to fulfill God's will, our situation as parents would be ideal because in so doing we would have allowed them to become instruments in the hands of God. Then, we would neither count on them, nor seek in them illusory reliance; instead, all of our expectations would be directed toward the Creator. He, Himself, could take care of us, whether through our children, other people, or other circumstances.

Each one of us has God as our Father. If we were open to this truth, then our food would also be to fulfill God's will. Our lives would become the best testimony for our children and for our grandchildren.

If parents, educators, and all the people to whom the faith of our children is entrusted do not live by faith and hope (in terms of allowing God's plans to be fulfilled) then to a great degree they limit His designs for others. If they are unable to see the things not visible to the naked eye, and if they are incapable of expecting things not yet present, then the pragmatism of their actions will be useless. Obviously, we cannot deny the fact that everything has its practical aspect, but these aspects mean nothing if they are without a supernatural dimension.

God truly desires that we anticipate, with faith and hope, the fulfillment of His plans toward our environment and us. Therefore, we should always look upon our dear ones, as well as those who are away from the faith, as God looks upon them in His mercy. God looks at them as saints, even though they may convert in a year, maybe in ten years, or even – as in the case of the Good Thief – only at the last hours of their lives. The best way for us to help others on their way to conversion is to better appreciate God's purpose connected to their lives, rather than trying to rely on them excessively.

It is crucial for us to place our reliance on God. At the same time, we must cooperate with His grace and anticipate, with great hope, what we have not yet received, but which we deeply believe is in accordance with God's designs. In this way the results of our reliance on God can also be the salvation of others.

PART TWO

WHEN OUR ILLUSORY RELIANCES FALL APART

There you go again, desiring riches and possessions! To lean on these things is like leaning on a piece of red hot iron; it will always leave its little scar. We must lean on nothing, even in the case of those things which we have reason to believe might help us in the spiritual life. It is then that we are seeking only the truth which consists in having neither desire for nor hope of enjoyment. How happy we are when we have reached that stage.

ST. THÉRÈSE OF THE CHILD JESUS
A Memoir of My Sister St. Thérèse

Is it possible for a human being – this creature who fabricates illusions, which then in turn help him to function and to live – to find true reliance? Our faith proclaims that God is the only One to guarantee this. Before a human heart leans totally on God, however, it has to experience the anguish connected to illusions falling apart. It also has to undertake the difficult task of avoiding human reliances. The goal of our lives is to allow Christ to possess us completely for Himself so that He will become everything for us.

CHAPTER 6

THE DECEPTIVE LIGHT OF HUMAN LOVE

Human beings seek love throughout their lives. False love, however, is so similar to true love that we can easily be deceived by it. When the illusions of false love fall apart, we remain deeply wounded and filled with bitterness.

BITTERNESS AND ILLUSIONS

St. Thérèse of the Child Jesus, describing her own life, showed us her unique intuitiveness when she spoke about the consequences of being immersed in the flame of fake love:

> How can I thank Jesus for making me find *only bitterness in earth's friendships!*" With a heart such as mine, I would have allowed myself to be taken and my wings to be clipped, and then how would I have been able to *"fly and be at rest?"* How can a heart given over to the affection of creatures be intimately united with God? . . . I have seen so many souls, seduced by this *false light,* fly like poor moths and burn their wings,

and then return to the real and gentle light of Love that gives them new wings which are more brilliant and delicate, so that they can fly toward Jesus, that Divine Fire "which burns without consuming." Ah! I feel it! Jesus knew I was too feeble to be exposed to temptation; perhaps I would have allowed myself to be burned entirely by the *misleading light* had I seen it . . . .[12]

We are so preoccupied with finding acceptance and understanding among humans. So often we resemble moths that fly blindly toward the delusory flame of false love. It is from this attitude that most of our dramatic experiences come.

Someone who, like a moth, clings to the flame of human love, who seeks this reliance and actually begs for this flame, receives only the world's recompense. Human love will always remain a mere substitute for the love for which a human heart truly searches. Such a person will have to withdraw from this flame, with burned wings and a burned-out soul, for human love cannot fill him with true happiness. As a result, a special place meant for God is destroyed. The Creator cannot in any measure be united with a soul in which a human person reigns.

PRETENSES TOWARD OTHER PEOPLE

What is evident in our relationships with others is a natural tendency to await mutuality as a reciprocal response to some goodness that we exercise toward them. Seeking reliance on

---

[12] St. Thérèse of Lisieux, *Story of a Soul*, 83.

human mutuality really is chasing after a mirage. It cannot substitute as a useful means to fulfill our true needs and longings. Sooner or later we will notice that our reliance on human mutuality brings us only a temporary sense of relief, and in time, we may come to realize that it is similar to poison because it is unable to truly resolve what is at the heart of our problems.

When we help someone we count on the mutuality of that person, that the person will reciprocate our care or our sacrifice. This becomes our expectation of our spouse, of our children, of our family, friends and coworkers. We forget that in reality it is **God who helps others through us**; we are not helping them. Each one of us is only an instrument in the hands of the Creator, to whom all praise and thanksgiving are due. This does not mean that we are not to be thankful to someone who has been kind to us. Gratitude is important and necessary, but it belongs first of all to God, only secondarily to another human being.

Our pretenses toward others often go beyond God's plans. Through these pretenses we count on something that can be extremely dangerous for us, destructive and catastrophic in its consequences. If we truly did not count on others and instead counted only on God and His will, we would then have no pretenses toward anyone who did not help us in the way we expected of them. We would understand that another person could not help us if God did not will it. Conversely, to expect this kind of help and to count on something that does not exist is equal to leaning on an illusion.

In the meantime, we have plenty of hidden pretenses and regrets toward people who do not meet our expectations. We are permeated with bitterness and a sense of loneliness due to these unanswered pretenses. Frequently our unfulfilled pretenses are connected to our anxiety. This anxiety is a sign that we do not have the posture of a poor in spirit. False reliance is present not only in relationships with people who are sympathetic toward us and who help us with joy, but also with those who repeatedly disappoint us and about whom we say we cannot rely. In either situation we may hinder God from being present in our lives.

Isn't it true that we should see in this suffering a very precious gift in the light of faith? Shouldn't we be thankful to God for the fact that we cannot count on anybody's help against His will?

If we want to taste, in a small way, the virtue of humility and to be – as St. John of the Cross says – in contempt of our own things and ourselves,[13] we must fight decisively against our pretenses toward other people and against our expectations for their gratefulness or mutuality. We cannot count, then, on the fact that some of our dear ones will surround us with care and attention when we are in need.

---

[13] "The second precaution against the world concerns temporal goods. To free yourself truly of the harm stemming from this kind of good and to moderate the excess of your appetite, **you should abhor all manner of possessions and not allow yourself to worry about these goods, neither for food, nor for clothing, nor for any other created thing, nor for tomorrow,** and direct this care to something higher – to seeking the kingdom of God (seeking not to fail God); and the rest, as His Majesty says, will be added unto us [Mt. 6:33], for he who looks after the beasts will not be forgetful of you. By this practice you will attain silence and peace in the senses." John of the Cross *Precautions* (trans. Kieran Kavanaugh and Otilio Rodriguez in *The Collected Works of St. John of the Cross* [Washington, DC: ICS Publications, 1991]) n. 7. Emphasis added by author.

Only God for sure will take care of us because He loves us. But He will do so in a perfect way from His point of view, and therefore from the point of view of love. Our loving Heavenly Father will always give us what is best for us, even if that is suffering or death. After all, everything that happens to us during our lives constitutes a meeting with the loving Presence of our God.

THE POISON OF ILLUSORY RELIANCE

Any human benevolence, shown to us against God's will, may become **poison** for us. When St. Peter told Jesus: "God forbid, Lord! No such thing shall ever happen to you," (Mt 16:22) certainly he wanted to show concern and kindness to his Divine Friend; he wanted to give Jesus psychological support. Subsequently, the words: "Get behind me, Satan! . . . You are thinking not as God does, but as human beings do," (Mt 16:23) precisely classify this deed of St. Peter. This is an example of how human benevolence shown against God's will can be compared to 'satanic' actions, even if it is clothed in the beautiful robes of concern and care. In actuality, it is capable of being destructive – a spiritual poison in a very dangerous form.

It behooves us to be certain that those with whom we are in relationships want only to do God's will; that they will not go against God's will in any way. When what we receive from others is the simple carrying out of God's will, only then will our spiritual lives not be wounded or destroyed. It is only God's will that has a healing impact at all times and only His will that can become a true source of reliance for us and a rescue for our souls. Every situation constitutes something that is best for us even if it is difficult to accept, for example, when somebody who is doing God's will refuses to offer us help. This desire of the Creator, who loves us infinitely, is always an expression of His purest love directed toward us.

In the meantime, because we are sinful and weak we often desire the poison of exultation and lean on our illusions. From this desire springs our hidden perverse longing for others to take care of us in order to satisfy our egoism, even when it means that we are going against God's will. Our egoism is hungry for this kind of food, even though we know that it is poisonous. When we do receive it, the effect, unfortunately, is always the same – it closes us to the truth about ourselves and once again we fall.

How are we to respond when God reminds us, once again, that we are full of pretenses toward other people, that we are leaning on illusions, and that we are weak and sinful? Furthermore, what are we to do when we are overwhelmed with the greed of human reliances that is poisoning our souls? Fortunately, there is a very helpful medicine for this condition. We have to try to stand in truth and admit the following before God: *My problem is based on the fact that I am filled with the pride of pretenses. I constantly expect mutuality and love from other people instead of counting only on You – this bitterness and regret that is filling my heart comes from unfulfilled expectations.* And, then, with ever increasing humility and faith, we have to frequently repeat: *Thank You, Lord, that You love me as such, that You embrace me as such, Lord Jesus.*

THE GRACE OF NOT HAVING RELIANCES

St. Thérèse considered it a **grace** that she was unable to find reliance on another person. She said: "How can I thank Jesus for making me find '*only bitterness in earth's friendships!*'"[14] It did not get in the way of her love that she showed toward her father and sisters. She was able to love her family most dearly, but at the same time she was free from any attachment toward them.

When she joined the Carmelites to dedicate herself to Jesus, she left behind her father – the one whom she liked to call "King," the one who loved and understood her, who was not only her guardian but also her dearest friend. Looking at this situation in human terms is difficult because she **left him** at the time when he was becoming disabled and dependent on the care of others. Soon after this time he became seriously ill, experiencing an extremely debilitating disease that made him dependent on others. This dependency was humiliating for him because he was in need of special assistance.

The attitude of St. Thérèse toward the illness of her father shows us that this very sensitive, young girl was detached from human ties with her father. She was detached from an illusory reliance on him. She loved him in a supernatural way, seeing through the eyes of faith a future saint in him. Moreover, she knew that the only real reliance for her father would be Christ – and therefore she prayed persistently for the grace of holiness for him.

---

[14] St. Thérèse of Lisieux, *Story of a Soul*, 83.

St. Thérèse's faithfulness toward God's will in connection to her dearly beloved father calls to our mind Mary. The Mother of Jesus did not attempt, as we would do in our human ways, to assist her son in suffering. She did not become like the man from Cyrene carrying the Cross to Golgotha. Mary accompanied Jesus, of course, but in a way perfectly united with God's will, fulfilling the design of the Creator toward Her as the Mother of His Son and the future Mother of all humanity. Since that time, Mary's relationship to Her Son has been for each Christian an ideal model for all human relationships.

CHAPTER 7

THE DECEIVING POWER OF THE HUMAN 'I'

Original sin wounded our human nature by bringing to the soul this desire that has become the echo of temptation, and to which our first parents succumbed: "You will be like gods" (Gen 3:5). Ever since the original sin, our aspiration toward transcendence is misguided toward exceeding the boundary of our own abilities. Instead of desiring the might of God within us, we try to rely on our own ego, which often proves to be only an illusion.

During the purifications of the dark night, our dear God strips us of this illusion and allows us to encounter His own might, which more clearly discloses our powerlessness. Through our daily experiences we are convinced about the blessed essence of this fragility, the human 'I'. These experiences may be our fear about the future (which is seen without God), the limitations of our mind and memory, or even what appears to be transitory – that on which we used to build our system of security.

THE ANGUISH OF OUR FUTURE SEEN WITHOUT GOD

When the goods of this world cease to be a source of reliance for us, we can reach a point where we have the sense of losing control over our lives, as did the Apostles during the storm on the sea (see Mk 4:35-41). They certainly attempted to pray and to overcome this great force by the power of their own hands, but, they still were unable to rely on themselves or their boat. Filled with fear, they doubted the possibility of a rescue; it appeared to them that they were sinking.

Frequently, during the time of purifications, when our reliances fall apart, we also react with fear. Since we usually realize that these difficult experiences are God's interventions in our lives, our desire to battle against them does not have to be shown directly. On the other hand, if these difficulties cause us to be anxious or discouraged, it means that we are questioning the very act of Redemption, brought about through the suffering and total denudation of our Lord.

At the root of this exaggerated concern about our future lies a questioning of our **hope in God,** of the fact that He Himself will take care of our tomorrow as He took care of our yesterday and our today. After all, God alone always was, is now, and will forever remain our only real support.

When we plan our future in the realm of our reason, unenlightened by faith, we are not taking into account the involvement of our omnipotent Father and His answer for the situations in which we find ourselves. Sometimes, then, it appears as if we are thinking like creatures who can determine our own futures. Is this not the truth about us?

Our Lord Jesus very strongly warns us against being preoccupied about the future (see Mt 6:34), even when our preoccupations about the future keep entering our minds. At the same time, it is true that during the time of purification our thinking about the future can haunt us, especially when we do not see any hope for ourselves in specific areas of our lives. During that time, we tend to believe that everything is lost and that we are doomed to a slow death. This gives birth to fear and to the desire to run away. Often, our repeated reaction to losing our reliances is to withdraw into our own small world. Depending on the development of our spiritual lives, and on the type of our personality and interests, this withdrawal can take different forms, but it is always a sign that we are still attempting to seek reliance apart from God.

On our road toward communion with Jesus we must keep in mind that these denudations are not subject to our control and our preferences. Our Lord is totally free as to how He chooses to purify us. It is possible that we, on our own, increase our suffering and anxiety by an inappropriate attitude toward the world – toward the present, the future and even the past.

Having an exaggerated concern about the future and forgetting about the intervention of God in our lives amounts to ingratitude – stepping on the gifts that made us beloved children of our Heavenly Father, surrounded constantly with His care. We question the fatherly love of God when our thinking about the future brings about sadness, discouragement and anxiety. Therefore, this exaggerated concern about the future not only causes psychological distress, but also spiritual anxiety arising from our lack of reliance on God's Providence.

A GLOVE THROWN TO US BY THE EVIL SPIRIT

Our discouragement and sadness, which occur when we fall into the temptation of an exaggerated concern about the future, show us very clearly that God is not present in this experience. This kind of thinking occurs as a 'deed' in which, unfortunately, the evil spirit often participates as well. Therefore, the words of our Savior: "Get behind me, Satan! You are an obstacle to me. You are thinking not as God does, but as human beings do," (Mt 16:23) can also be applied to us.

When we are concerned about the future in an exaggerated way, we are actually being submissive to Satan in the same way as was St. Peter. After hearing from Jesus that He was going to suffer and die, St. Peter reacted decisively with opposition: "God forbid, Lord! No such thing shall ever happen to you" (Mt 16:22). There was Peter standing in confrontation of the approaching suffering and death of his

Master, and connecting his Master's fate with his own suffering, he wanted to take care of it in a purely human way.

This temptation of exaggerated concern about the future inherently questions our hope that God will actually take care of us. And when we are beset with **temptations against hope, faith, or purity**, we **should not**, as St. Maximilian Mary Kolbe warned us, **fight** against them **directly**.[15] These temptations present a glove thrown to us by Satan himself, and they are a challenge from him. The one who goes into battle with Satan determines in advance his own catastrophe, for he is trying to rely on himself, thinking that he is stronger than the evil spirit. The question arises: what should we do?

We simply have to imagine that someone is calling us to fight, someone much stronger and full of pride. However, if you know that you are unable to defeat him by yourself, it will be most profitable for you to leave the glove behind. In medieval times, for a knight to be ignored in such a fashion was considered the **ultimate disgrace**. Similarly, Satan will also be humiliated and conquered by this kind of disregard, by your **ignoring** of this **temptation**. Otherwise, he will try to weaken and destroy you, tempting you with thoughts about your future and leading you to greater sadness, discouragement and despair.

---

[15] "When there comes a temptation against faith, against the sixth commandment, against hope, etc., then do not wrestle with it but rather turn away the thought to something else. It is important to turn the thought from the temptation immediately. Calmly, but immediately." Maximilian Mary Kolbe, *Konferencje Świetego Maksymiliana Marii Kolbego* (Conferences of Saint Maximilian Mary Kolbe), (Niepokalanów: 1983), 308.

QUESTIONING OF EXAGGERATED CONCERNS

God does not expect us to struggle with exaggerated concerns and with thoughts about our future. Oh, how happy is the one who in the simplicity of his heart looks at his present life situation and does not get ahead of himself. In his thoughts about the future, he sees that it does not depend on him, but lies totally in the hands of God. Moreover, the examples of various saints confirm our conviction that God's intervention can be so powerful that even death by terrible tortures can be permeated with His presence. In this way, a person can be united with the One who shows His presence in the most tender love.

During the period of purifications, our active renunciation should be concentrated on constant questioning of the exaggerated concern that we have about our future and the future of those who are entrusted to us. When we experience the temptations to be rebellious, fearful or discouraged, we have to readily **admit** to our enslavement to human reliances, and our lack of faith, while simultaneously calling upon God's mercy with trust. In this way, Jesus will lean over to look upon our misery and He will take upon Himself our denudation, overcoming barriers that are insurmountable for us.

We also can defend ourselves against this exaggerated concern through acts of faith, hope and trust, even when these acts seem to be totally unsuccessful. Regardless of that, we should call upon our loving God – as the blind man from Jericho, as Peter who was drowning, or as the Apostles during the storm on the lake: *Lord, rescue me! Jesus, have pity on me!* We should pray in this way, in order that He Himself will prevent us from trampling on God's love. We should cry out: *Lord, You see that I am not only being unfaithful to You, but I also spread my sadness and my thinking in human terms to others. Lord, please rescue me!*

In this way, lack of faith, sadness, even discouragement as well as rebelliousness, are not definite obstacles on the path to sanctity. These obstacles exist only when we give up calling upon the depth of the Sacrifice of Christ.

THE PURIFICATION OF OUR REASON AND MEMORY

It is understandable that in our daily existence we are led by the promptings of our mind, knowledge, and gained experience, which substitute as a source of reliance for us. God permits this to happen until a certain stage of our interior lives.

Gradually, He may want us to begin to rely more and more on Him alone, and in this way give up our illusions that are linked to other reliances. In order to accept the collapse of our false reliances, we need to question everything that, up to this point, we have considered to be the basis of our existence, and that we have always accepted without a doubt.

Our minds, however, might not agree to this process. Our memories may even protest, suggesting to us various experiences from the past, from which we conclude decisively that the losing of these reliances will lead to a total disaster. Minds not enlightened by faith, and memories not cleansed can become sources of doubt, opposition, and even rebelliousness toward God's demands. And, precisely because of this fact, purification of mind and memory is needed.[16]

It is therefore important that we desire to undertake acts of renunciation, constantly denying ourselves in order to become increasingly more open to our loving Father's gifts. God wants us to question our own judgments and assessments, allowing Him to expose the false preoccupations, illusions, and pretenses contained in them. Thus, we will stand before Him with open hearts and souls, with a will truly ready to follow Him. What is most important here is our interior disposition – our willingness to question our own ways of thinking. As long as we are able to do this, we will discover in ourselves the disposition to follow God's voice.

God desires that we be more united to Him, and that we lead fuller lives of faith, relying solely on His power and His love. This would undoubtedly be in complete contradiction to our attachments and the whole system of illusory reliances that are given to us by the spirit of this world. The deeper our reliances are rooted in our experiences from the past and in our way of thinking, so too the deeper purification of our mind and memory is needed.

---

[16] St. John of the Cross stresses that on the way to union with God, the mind has to be purified from its support which constitutes everything it can easily understand and comprehend. Also, the mind has to be "inwardly pacified and silenced, and supported by faith alone." John of the Cross *Ascent of Mount Carmel* (trans. Kieran Kavanaugh and Otilio Rodriguez in *The Collected Works of St. John of the Cross* [Washington, DC: ICS Publications, 1991]) 2.9.1.

This, of course, involves a certain degree of suffering. We are not to be afraid of this suffering because it is our merciful Father who leads us through different tests of faith with great tenderness. These tests are meant to free us from relying on our illusions, that we may be more united with our loving God. These tests are given so that we can expand our vision, looking beyond that to which our limited mind and experiences point.

BLESSED WEAKNESSES

Each one of us wants the assurance of being strong, fit and capable of deciding our faith. As a result, we are afraid of all weakness – physical, psychological and spiritual – because we think that these weaknesses render us unable to live. In the meantime, when God takes away our false reliances and the realization of our powerlessness intensifies, we are led to a deeper reliance on Him.

In order for this deeper reliance on God to occur, however, we must be disappointed by all of the other sources of reliance we have had and lose our illusions connected to them. We should not be surprised that as we go deeper into our spiritual lives our capability to fight off stress and humiliations decreases. We feel more powerless when faced with the problems of life that God puts in front of us. Our Savior demands a deeper communion with Him, and that comes only when we are beset by problems and events, which lead us to the realization that we can find our reliance only in Him.

The weakness that we are so afraid of, in essence, becomes our blessing and a tremendous gift. As our psychological endurance decreases, we lose our reliance on ourselves. What follows next is that we become aware that this is an illusion that we are able to deal with problems on our own. Because of this awareness, we are forced to **beg for mercy**, to seek reliance on God. Subsequently, a unique opportunity occurs – God's grace penetrates our hearts. Then Jesus can use us as His instruments, at least to some degree. It greatly increases the efficacy of our involvement because a special intervention of God's Providence is triggered.

God will definitely work miracles in our lives if we allow Him to enter our lives, at least to some extent. The best situations, then, from a spiritual sense, are those in which, in the midst of our weakness and powerlessness, we begin to beg for God's mercy, being convinced that the Creator loves us as we are.

THE 'MIGHT' THAT PASSES AWAY

If we are still capable and strong in certain areas of our lives, we need to acknowledge that this is only a temporary state. Being in good physical condition, being in good spirits psychologically, or being in great 'spiritual condition' (our own perception) – all this is fleeting. Everything gradually has to be taken away from us some day so that we can cling only to God. Our powerlessness and a sense of total dependence on our Creator in all areas of our lives should become a norm for us – when we are completely permeated by the words of Jesus who said: "Without me you can do nothing" (Jn 15:5). **Nothing** – this means not even the smallest thing.

Taking advantage of our physical, psychological and spiritual weakness leads us to humbly beg for our communion with Christ. This state really demands great faith. If this feeling of helplessness is only related to a few aspects of our lives, we should, in the spirit of humility, recognize that it is because our faith is so weak. Our **weak faith** prevents us from being more exposed to different tests of helplessness, tests that are really God beckoning us to rely on Him and not on ourselves.

CHAPTER 8

PURIFICATION OF HUMAN RELATIONS

W e can close ourselves off from God when we immerse ourselves in the spirit of the world and seek reliance on things or persons. We seek help from others, become attached to them and begin to almost worship them – through this we may discover how we have become lost in our own world. Likewise, we can place ourselves in the dangerous situation of provoking others to be lost in the world by seeking reliance on us, being attached to us and showing us respect, honor or even worship – thereby increasing our state of being lost in the world.

To be released from this trap, we must look at the world through a different perspective, and be more open to God. We will then be led to a deeper union with Him. This takes place when we begin to discover His presence in things offered to us, and in people He places on the path of our lives, with whom God wants us to establish various kinds of supernatural ties.

Is it possible, though, for even the most wonderful and spiritual person to become, on his own, a true reliance for us?

WHEN WE FORGET ABOUT THE GIVER

St. John of the Cross warns us that the soul, which is attached to other creatures, is completely incapable of union with the infinite being of God.[17] **It is not possible.**

Therefore, God has to purify us from all human relationships that are hindering us from Him; this purification can happen either here on earth or in purgatory. It is our Lord who desires to be more united with us, and He urges us to be cleansed of all blood relations and friendships.[18] This process also happens in marriage. Because of this purification process, we can be sure that a time will come when both husband and wife will become very lonely and completely misunderstood by the other spouse.

We forget that the person whom we love is only an instrument in the hands of our loving God; he is God's gift for us and our help on the way to sanctity. If a soul allows

---

[17] John of the Cross Ascent of Mount Carmel (Kavanaugh) 1.4.4.

[18] St. John of the Cross stresses the necessity to purify the natural feelings toward relatives and friends, so they do not constitute an obstacle for complete reliance on God: "The first is that you should have an equal love for and an equal forgetfulness of all persons, whether relatives or not, and withdraw your heart from relatives as much as from others, and in some ways even more for fear that flesh and blood might be quickened by the natural love that is ever alive among kin, and must always be mortified for the sake of spiritual perfection. Regard all as strangers, and you will fulfill your duty toward them better than by giving them the affection you owe God." John of the Cross Precautions (Kavanaugh) 5-6.

another creature to be attached to him, then the gift becomes more important than the Giver; he obscures God and plays the role of an idol. The soul then becomes like a spoiled child who, upon receiving a beautiful gift, forgets totally about the one who gave the gift to him. The child turns his back to the giver and focuses his attention on the new toy, completely ignoring the giver and failing to even say "thank you." If we do not accept such ungrateful behavior in our human relationships, then we should be aware that it truly offends and wounds God – the Father who gives us everything through the person of His Son, who makes an offering of His life for us.

Every gift must remind us about the Giver, must cause us to focus on God alone and not obscure Him. This also applies to human kindness or cordiality, the gift of friendship, the gift of marital love, or the showing of care and concern in our relationships with children. When our emotions are concentrated upon persons who are only gifts of God's love, in essence we are not properly appreciating either the Giver or the gift; we destroy our friendship with God, and we show Him disdain. In this case the person who is dear to us, instead of becoming our help on the way to sanctity, becomes our stumbling block. When we adore this person, like a moth, we fly toward the flame that will destroy us.

For many years, without any harm to our soul, we may take advantage of the psychological reliance that comes from a person who is dear to us, if we remember that it is God who offers us these sources of reliance, and if we remember to cooperate with God's grace. Then our world will not collapse even if our Lord decides to take this person away from us once His plan has been fulfilled regarding the role of that person in our lives. We will actually see in this situation a plan of God's love and consequently **another gift** from Him.

Jesus, during His public ministry, spoke about Himself in this way: "Foxes have dens and birds of the sky have nests, but the Son of Man has nowhere to rest his head" (Lk 9:58). Our Savior spoke these words – which do not have to be interpreted solely as the lack of a stable place to live – during the time when the Apostles were still totally dedicated to Him. These words may indicate that following Christ is connected with the relinquishing of our human reliances, which we seek in our relationships with our dear ones.

TWO KINDS OF PURIFICATIONS

If we treat people as a support in themselves then our relationships with them become false and filled with illusions. If God wants to lead us into a spiritual desert and attempt to make even a part of these illusions evaporate, we will undergo deep frustrations.

During this time of denudation, we frequently will experience a sense of loneliness and rejection from other people; in fact, everybody can let us down. And so, we might feel cheated, hurt and betrayed when we begin to lose the support of persons who had previously shown us kindness and in whom we had previously trusted.

During this process of purification God simultaneously might allow those who relied on us to also be disappointed with us. In this way we can experience a **double purification** – first in relation with those on whom we relied and second with those who relied on us.

All these experiences will be very difficult to handle, especially when we realize that by our own efforts we are incapable of always relying on others in the way that God wants us to. Our Merciful Father does not want us to be sad and full of bitterness. What He truly desires is that we admit to the truth about ourselves and that we bring this truth to Him. So, kneeling before our Father we can tell Him with humility and trust: *I am blind to Your love Lord. I am sold into slavery to sin and my inappropriate relation to Your gifts, Lord, only hinders me from You. Lord, I do not want to crucify You by adoring another person, or by becoming a hindrance for another who will not see You. I do not want to forget about You, my Savior. Therefore, I beg You to come to my rescue, look kindly upon my misery, be united to me, and in me and for me*[19] *adore God present in my life through other persons.*

---

[19] The expression "in me and for me" should be understood in the context of the words Jesus addressed to St. Margaret Mary Alacoque: I want "that from this time on you may live only the life of a Man-God, that is to say…that you may live as if not living, but…allowing me to live in you. Because I am your life and you will only live in me…I want you to act as not acting: letting me act and operate in you and for you, leaving to me the care about everything. You should not have your own will and, by not having any, allow me to want for you in everything and everywhere." St. Marguerite-Marie, *Sa vie par elle-même,* 65 (Paris: 1979), 94.

DIFFICULTY OF THE HEART IN AVOIDING
HUMAN RELIANCE

How can we avoid our interpersonal relationships from becoming a hindrance in our union with God? First of all, our loving God wants us to admit that we are enslaved to our human desires, to kindness, to remembrance, and to acceptance. God wants us to desire to see this problem within ourselves and to admit it before Him.

Undoubtedly, what is also needed is our effort to take steps in this process of not seeking attachments, to avoid occasions that will awaken attachments in ourselves or others. What is essential here is some effort of the heart. We must diligently try to avoid all kinds of attachments so that we will be freed from them.

Also, in our relationships, prudence must dictate to us that we keep a healthy distance from others. Of course, sometimes we have to forgo this disposition because of a person's psychological or spiritual fragility, but it is always better that we keep some distance from others; especially those who are immature enough to become attached to us. Upon discerning each situation in our conscience, we should not forget about our own enslavement to others and therefore, we should beg Jesus that He, Himself, will direct our endeavors and our ways.

Our Lord Jesus Christ, in His contacts with the Apostles, did show favor to some. For example, He showed more affection to John than to the others; but finally He had to leave them all so that they could receive the Consoler – the Holy Spirit.

We should not deceive ourselves by thinking that merely theoretical knowledge about human attachments is sufficient enough for us to live it. Therefore, we should not be surprised by our continual failures in this field. We should not forget that our Redeemer does not come to the healthy ones but rather to the sick, to those who need a physician. Being the Divine Physician, our Redeemer alone can heal us from our sins. If, full of hope, we continue to persevere in bringing to Him all the different aspects of our misery, then one day the moment will arrive when He will bend over us in response to our trustful begging for healing, finally uniting with us completely.

GOD'S INSTRUMENT PUT ON OUR PATH

Saints, upon losing the source of reliance on their dear ones, entrusted themselves to God without reservation. During the dark night, however, even they accepted spiritual help from persons whom God put in their way. Our Heavenly Father wants us to find in others – especially in those who are instruments in His hands – the source of reliance that He gives us through them.

Therefore, during the process of purification, then, we can gain friendship in a spiritual sense to replace human bonds, friendship by which Christ Himself will surround us with His care and through another person will give us His own support. We will not be able, though, to seek merely a human reliance on this person.

It may turn out to be very difficult to accept the reliance Christ gives us through another human strictly on the spiritual level, especially when the relationship was previously a human friendship. Spiritual friendship will not satisfy the expectations we may normally have in our friendships. Therefore, we should try to **separate the personal characteristics** from the person's characteristics **that God wants to create in us**. Our Creator, first of all, will try to fulfill and realize His own purpose for us through this person, and in this sense, the person put on the path of our life as God's instrument can become a support for us. Until this person becomes a saint, however, he can give us only a small degree of what God wants to bestow on us. Only someone who is fully united with Christ can give us everything that God intends for us.

When practicing acts of renunciation, we must devoutly pray for the grace of being able to look with the eyes of faith on everything that we experience from other people. If we do not have enough faith, then we must not be surprised if we do not receive help from someone through whom God wants to give us His own support. This outlook of faith will help us to understand that another person, by himself, is not capable of helping us and in every moment can wound us very painfully. Seeing our faith, God can grant graces to His special instrument who, despite his numerous imperfections, can nonetheless become an extension of God's helping hand for us. All of the reliances given to us from God function in this way.

BEFORE WHOM ARE WE CONFESSING OUR SINS?

A key role in our openness to grace is played by our prayerful posture of faith before the sacrament of Reconciliation. When we go to confession, we usually have to wrestle with a hidden pharisaism, very deeply rooted in us. We do not completely believe in the presence of Christ in the priest who hears our confession, and when we treat this person humanly, we are trying to hide the abyss of our evil. We do not trust that when we fully admit to Christ's presence we can witness the miracle of transformation. We behave like the criminal before the tribunal who is manipulating the truth in an attempt to secure a lesser punishment for his crime.

It is not so important, however, if the confessor discovers our misery or if he does not entirely do so because God sees our misery as it is. We come to God, not to the priest, to confess our sins and to receive the grace of forgiveness. We confess before Christ and we meet with Him in the sacrament of Reconciliation. Some saints had the practice of confessing their sins as if they were admitting them directly to Jesus. The most important thing during confession is not the form, regulated by the Church, but rather, if we see Christ. Do we want to rely on Jesus, or are we seeking a human reliance on our confessor?

If this posture of faith dominates during our confession, then nobody else will exist for us but Jesus Christ, to whom we come and before whom we stand, with the realization of our deep misery and perverseness. If we have this posture of faith, it is possible for all kinds of pharisaic endeavors to be blocked in us. Then we will be able to be more open to the grace of forgiveness and to fully take advantage of it. In this case, our cooperation with God's grace will look completely different in our lives, and our everyday existence will be more fruitful.

SUPERNATURAL FRIENDSHIP

A different kind of perspective is required in order to build supernatural relationships with other people. If, when looking at a person dear to us, we attempt to see in him God's gift, then we will concentrate our attention on the One who gives us this gift. Then we will discover that our loyalty toward our friend should first be subject to our loyalty to God, even if our chosen action appears to be a rejection of this gift of friendship.

A true loyalty to God sometimes requires – depending on God's will – that we leave our friend in need, refusing to give him external support in the forms of kindness and help. The most important thing for him is that we cease to hinder God, and allow this person, through faith, to seek reliance only in our Creator. Likewise, our spiritual friends, whom God has put on the path of our lives, may deal in a similar way with us. As His instruments, God may demand that from them.

Of course, the example for us is our Lord, Jesus Christ who, by ascending into Heaven, left behind, in a sense, His beloved disciples. He deprived them of contact with Himself, the attachment that would be perceived by their senses, forcing them to rely on Him through faith.

The following temptations will always come back to us: to lean on emotional contacts with others, to desire human understanding, and to believe that other persons will be truly faithful to us. In the meantime, a spiritual friend can remain in spiritual darkness. God sometimes allows a lack of communication to exist in such situations – and this barrier will be most difficult for us to overcome. Quite often we will have difficulties accepting these kinds of experiences, and we will still accept living in our illusions – filled with hope for human understanding and for close friendship. This can be a source of suffering and painful disappointment for us. After all, every human relationship is based on the assumption that this friend will not let us down in our need. This assumption is fiction. **God** is the only **faithful One who will not let us down**. He may, however, allow a person, who is in agreement with His purposes, to remain faithful to us, only in accordance with His will.

When God detaches us from a human reliance whom He used up to this point, He shows us very clearly how weak this human instrument is. He does this as if He is trying to tell us: See, I am the only reliance for you and not this person.

Thus, while facing various problems and difficulties, it will be most appropriate if we try most of all to **rely directly on** God through our prayer and the acts of faith, hope and love. It is possible that God may want us to seek reliance on Him **indirectly** through a person in our life, who may become the extension of God's helping hand. However, when seeking support in this friend, who is given to us by God, and when asking this person for help, we should still rely directly on God who in this situation is acting through His instrument.

If we try, through the gift of friendship, to see and discover our Father, the Giver, then we will come closer to the flame that was described by St. Thérèse – the flame "'which burns without consuming.'"[20] The flame of God's love is the only flame that does not wound us, but rather, renews us. His flame enables us to fly toward Him higher and higher – so that through this immersion in Him we can be transformed.

The Mother of God, being immersed in the flames of God's love, was so transformed that she looked in a supernatural way on everything and everybody; she thought, perceived and loved in His way. For us as well, the most important thing is to fall in love with God and **only with Him**. In this way, by being more united to Him, who is the only One that loves us eternally, we too may be immersed forever in the transforming flame of His love.

---

[20] St. Thérèse of Lisieux, *Story of a Soul*, 83.

PART THREE

BEING LIBERATED FROM ILLUSIONS

Try that all things become nothing to you and you become nothing to them.

ST. JOHN OF THE CROSS
Special Counsels

T hanks to the purifying action of grace and our cooperation with it, our attachments in the material and psychological realms, although they do not cease to exist, lose their magical glamour that previously attracted us and drew our greed. Of course, this does not mean that we are liberated from illusory reliances.

When God desires to draw us closer to Him, He gradually shows us the value of supernatural gifts. When this occurs, our gravity point shifts from the material and psychological realms to the spiritual realm, so that supernatural gifts become the new objects of our desire. Our distorted self-love feeds on everything and so this human greed shifts its hopes to something more subtle.

This situation can be portrayed as any or all of the following: seeking reliance on spiritual progress, living as a disguised Pharisee, or leaning on spiritual gifts as if they could be separated from the Divine Giver. These spiritual reliances, which are more subtle than the previous ones, are also more dangerous. Therefore, we must be more alert and also more open to the purifying love of God.

CHAPTER 9

ILLUSORY RELIANCE ON OUR OWN PERFECTION

S upernatural gifts are what become vital for the person who is trying to live the interior life. Such a person thinks that in this perspective of the journey to God the spiritual gifts make him *somebody* and that they assure him a *strong spiritual position*. But can we really determine our actual spiritual progress by these standards?

The person poor in spirit is the one who does not have any reliance other than God. Illusory reliances in the spiritual realm, which are constantly being generated by our self-love, prevent us from fulfilling the evangelical beatitudes and from living in communion with God. Our Lord, being a jealous God, wants to be united with the soul to the degree to which the soul is purified from attachments. This can occur only to the extent to which we make room for Him.

GRACES THAT WE TRY TO ATTRIBUTE TO OURSELVES

One of our most common reliances is a good self-image. Everyone wants to believe that he is good and think about himself in the best possible way, and to rely on this positive vision of himself. This reliance on our good self-image concerns not only our physical abilities, intellectual capabilities, or personality traits, but also our spiritual values.

When our Lord gets closer to us, His light enables us to see our imperfections and our faults more clearly. How do we react to this? Usually, at all cost, we want to change and improve ourselves, to get rid of our faults, to finally become 'different persons'.

But when we take a closer look at our desires for improvement, we notice that, in essence, what we seek is reliance on our own perfection. Our desire is to **conquer and possess** the interior capacity to do good so that we can rely on this.

When we dream about the fastest way to acquire this perfection based on the illusion that we can 'conquer God' through our own efforts, we then resemble a greedy rich person. We resemble someone, who having everything, still wants to possess one more thing. In this example, we desire yet more spiritual gifts.

Conversely, the person poor in spirit does not have anything and desires nothing. Such a person does not own either perfection or virtues. The process of becoming poor in spirit puts us on the road of unceasing openness to grace.

Then we will in each moment surrender to God's action, and humbly admit that every good thing born in us comes only from God.

In a humble person, there is no room to possess perfection, or to freely use any personal attributes or capabilities. This posture of the poor in spirit indicates a desire that is opposite from what was previously described. It indicates that Jesus can use us freely; that we can be at His total disposal with our whole body and soul.

Only this attitude of spiritual poverty can protect us from the temptation of attributing to ourselves graces that God wants to give us. It prevents us from desiring to possess the good, which God does through us and in us. To have this attitude, however, requires us to be poor in relation to everything we do and everything we have.

On the way to spiritual poverty you can become a true Christian, a good father or a loving wife only when you agree that you will never become the master of virtues nor have the interior disposition needed for such a state to happen. Moreover, you need to agree to accept the experiences that will reassure you that in yourself you are completely incapable of doing anything. Only then, through the deep conviction of your own incapability can the following attitude be born in you: the assurance that each time you entrust yourself to Jesus and allow Him to direct you without any hindrance, He alone will show, in you and through you, this exceptional care as a father, as a faithful wife, or a good Christian. This capability will never become your own possession on which you can lean.

During this journey toward spiritual poverty, the desire will be reborn in us to **possess** the capability of doing and of being good based on our own strengths and efforts. When this happens, God may grant us the **painful** grace of denudation from the illusions connected to these desires. Moreover, seeking the illusory reliance on possessing some kind of virtue can lead to the loss of this particular gift from God.

When we lose every illusion that we can be good Christians, parents, or spouses on our own, there will be born in us the prayer of trustful begging, wherein we ask God to direct us. It should not surprise us that we see increasingly more evil in ourselves as we progress in our spiritual lives, and that we discover how we need to rely more and more on God. This situation leads us to beg for mercy and, thanks to it, an authentic goodness can be generated in us, a goodness that does not belong to us, but rather to Christ, who is acting in us and through us. The road to this goodness leads to the deeper discovery of our own evil and the unending mercy of God, which is being poured upon us continuously.

USURPERS OF VIRTUES

We can even attribute faith and hope to ourselves – virtues given to us by God. We do not want to receive these virtues in the posture of humility, and in this way, these precious gifts become a source of reliance for us. Thus, faith and hope become an illusion and, at the same time, an **obstacle** toward fuller union with God.

Take, for example, the conviction that we are people of faith who truly believe in God and in everything that He reveals to us. This conviction may grow in us and be cherished for many years. This conviction comes from no other source than the pride of holding ourselves in high esteem. We continue on this way until God decides to purify us. If we have not questioned this illusory conviction with humility and if we have not turned to ask God to grant us faith, then we will never be able to truly rely on our faith. Can our own conviction that we are people of faith, a fictional illusion generated by our own pride, become a reliance for us?

God does not want us to rely on the **pride of possessing faith**, but rather, desires that we learn to rely on faith alone. Faith is, after all, a gift freely given to us by God, and we can never become owners of it. Even though we understand this, we remain like the pigs that trample upon the pearls of faith, feeling as if we are the masters and owners of our faith.

Only when our Lord puts us through this test of faith will we see how illusive is our conviction that we really have this virtue. We will begin to lose our reliance on the illusion that we are people of faith, an illusion full of the pride of holding ourselves in high esteem.

A similar illusory conviction derived from the **pride of our high esteem** is the conviction that we can lean on God in our lives, and that we truly trust our Heavenly Father. God may allow us to live for many years in this illusion, based on the positive feeling of experiencing trust, and on the remembrance of those moments when we very clearly experienced the care of God's Providence. During the time of purification, however, even this illusion can be questioned. At that time, we will discover how much distrust toward the Redeemer is in us.

The symptoms of lack of trust in God's love can be many and varied, depending on our character and also on how we have been wounded in our lives. One symptom is a lack of trust in our regular confessor. At a certain point in our spiritual lives we may discover that we truly are not able to give our confessor the trust he deserves. In this way we are forgetting that he is the person through whom Christ is present to us, constantly giving up His life for us.

When our Lord helps us to discover this sprouting seed of distrust, He does not want us to become sad about it. Instead He wants us, with humility, to bring it to His feet. Leaning on the sense of total helplessness and on the awareness of our own misery, which is clearly portrayed in our lack of trust toward Him, the One who is worthy of our ultimate trust, we can still call out to our Lord, begging Him to unite Himself to us. In this way, our distrust can be overcome; if He unites Himself to us, He will live in us and trust for us.[21]

---

[21] The expression "for us" should be understood in the context of the words Jesus addressed to St. Margaret Mary Alacoque. St. Marguerite-Marie, *Sa vie par elle-même*, 94.

WHEN WE WANT TO 'CAPTURE' THE GIFT OF PRAYER

When our God enters into our lives in a special way, we become like different persons. We may experience a certain ease in persevering at prayer, for example, during adoration of the Blessed Sacrament or in our meditation. Certain renunciations related to our daily reliances, may also be easy to undergo. What, then, should be our proper posture toward this state? Even though it may seem paradoxical, we should **be afraid** of this state. The most dangerous situations are those that can lead us to become possessive and attribute to ourselves those gifts that really are not ours. This certain ease at prayer is a gift from God, related to His specific plan, which we receive for a period of time. Unfortunately, we can waste this grace when we try to rely on it. St. John of the Cross highlights this: when the Holy Spirit comes to our soul and fills it with His delicate presence, the most fundamental mistake we can make is to try to maintain this state in ourselves, as if trying to 'capture' the action of God, making it our own possession.[22]

True reliance is not found in these gifts or graces, even if they are the most beautiful and spiritual. This feeling of security, which is built on religious practices, is an illusion. No practice can guarantee that we are on the proper spiritual road; therefore, no practice constitutes a genuine reliance. A true reliance can only come from God – who is the Giver of all gifts. If we put our trust in God's gifts instead of in the

---

[22] John of the Cross *The Dark Night* (trans. Kieran Kavanaugh and Otilio Rodriquez in *The Collected Works of St. John of the Cross* [Washington, DC: ICS Publications, 1991]) 1.9.6.

Giver Himself, then any gift separated from Him, becomes an illusion – even if the gift is prayer.

Upon discovering how inappropriate our posture is before God, we should say: *Only You, Lord, can allow me to pray with ease, to adore You in the Blessed Sacrament, or to talk to You. This miracle will escape from my hands, should I try to capture it. Only You can allow no greed of human reliance or impurity toward Your gifts to exist within me.*

A MAGICAL RELATIONSHIP TOWARD GOD'S GIFTS

As we grow in faith, we become aware that God, our Creator and Redeemer, unceasingly pours upon us His natural and supernatural gifts. We know this theoretically; in reality, however, we live as if the One who grants us these gifts does not exist.

By attributing these gifts of God to ourselves, we may make it impossible for God to grant us further graces. For our own good, He has to oppose our pride. Even such spiritual gifts as God's promises depend very much on our cooperation with grace. Unfortunately, too often we rely on God's words in a **magical way**; we assume that they can become a source of reliance for us, regardless of what the state of our life looks like.

St. John of the Cross, in his work *Ascent of Mount Carmel*, explains this posture and its implications by citing an example from the Old Testament. Referring to the first Book of Kings he describes how God, angered by Eli's attitude, withdrew His promise given to Eli's family: "Since the ministry of the priesthood is based on rendering honor and glory to God, God promised it to Eli's father forever. When Eli lacked zeal for the honor of God because, as God Himself complained, he gave more honor to his sons than to God, dissimulating their sins so as not to reprove them, the promise also failed [1 Sm. 3:13]. It would have been kept forever if their good service and zeal had been enduring." [23]

This passage clearly indicates that spiritual reliance can be very illusory if we assume a false attitude toward God. Eli the priest took advantage of God's gift without cooperating with His grace, so God withdrew His promise. This may happen to us as well, that we can waste the gift, the gift of God's promise, by forgetting about the One who bestowed this grace upon us – which God always bestows upon us for His greater glory.

EVIL FLOWING FROM THE SEPARATION OF THE GIFT FROM THE GIVER

The desire to become 'like God', to be in control of our lives and ourselves, is repeatedly generated in us. When we fall into this temptation, we want to rely on what we possess, on what we attribute to ourselves. We attempt to live as if we possess something, as if we can rely on something or somebody. In reality, we can rely only on God.

We can honestly say that we are slaves to 'looking at reality as if God did not exist'. We do not see the penetrating presence of our God. In contrast, everything that we come in

---

[23] John of the Cross *Ascent of Mount Carmel* (Kavanaugh) 2.20.4.

contact with seems to be so real and concrete, as if anything, by itself, could be our source of reliance. We leave such little space in our lives for contact with God because the things of this world absorb us so much.

We truly take advantage of God's mercy at every moment of our lives, and yet we do not show proper gratitude to our Creator. It is not difficult to find proof of this ingratitude. Which one of us really thanks God for the fact that we can breathe? Are we grateful to God for the fact that we are able to walk, or that we can think and speak? These are very fundamental things, but do we thank God for them? Perhaps we are taking advantage of these gifts, not thinking at all about the Giver, and so, this indicates that we are leaning only on the gifts and not on the One who has offered them to us. We do not have enough faith. Our lack of faith and our lack of gratitude are signs that we are, to a certain degree, enslaved by the evil in us.

Our will is often so weak that we may begin to doubt whether we really do have good will. Do we, in reality, want to lean on the things of this world, or do we truly want to live in God's presence and pray? Perhaps this "I want" is so weak in us that in certain situations we cannot really lean on God, the Giver of all gifts. Maybe we do want to lean on Him, but our sin lies in the fact that we want to be like God – we want to be the lords of ourselves.

When our Lord gradually strips us of our illusions and enlightens us with grace, we are able to begin to see our unfaithfulness more and more clearly. We do not have to be afraid of the moments when the Lord discloses to us that we are enslaved by illusory reliance and sin. Rather, the real danger lies in the situation when, upon becoming possessive of virtues, we do not turn to Jesus Christ because we are convinced that we are free and that God is not really the One whom we need. The person who sees himself as a slave should immediately run to the Redeemer in order to take advantage of the grace of freedom that was brought to us by Jesus on the Cross. So, then, we should place all of our illusions and temptations at His feet.

THE MIRAGE OF RELIANCE

God unceasingly grants us gifts and showers us with His graces; He expects **our posture to be one of faith**. In the meantime, we take these divine qualities, such as constancy and stability, and build our sense of security on them. We attribute our sense of security to the gifts God has given us rather than to God alone. We start to rely on these gifts. Leaning on gifts, detached from the Divine Giver, generates pride, which comes from the illusion of self-reliance. When this illusion evaporates, we will be exposed to very painful disappointments.

Imagine a very tired person who sees an armchair that is only a mirage. To his impaired senses, this chair appears to have substance, but in reality, the chair does not exist. The illusion becomes evident when the person tries to sit. Expecting to rest comfortably, the person painfully falls and is sadly disappointed.

The *Magnificat* also explains how God opposes prideful people. A prideful person builds his own greatness on various gifts that God has lavished on him. True greatness, however, is built on God alone. Here on Earth we will have to lose all of God's gifts, except the spiritual ones. At the moment of death we will stand before Him naked, stripped of all human reliances and totally at the disposal of His mercy.

CHAPTER 10

DISGUISED PHARISEE

W hen our Lord leads us along the road of spiritual life, we tend to have the following thought: "I am unlike them," who have not yet discovered God and who have not desired Him with their whole hearts. This disguised Pharisee will associate with us and because of him we will also need the graces of purification.

THE VAINGLORY

Each contact with God and the graces connected to that contact can become the source of vainglory (conceit) and hidden self-satisfaction, which consequently become a truly significant prey that feeds our spiritual pride. St. John of the Cross warned that we are not shielded from this danger even when we have a certain degree of acknowledgment of our own misery, or when we attribute graces to God, or when we thank Him and attempt to feel unworthy of these graces. This Doctor of the Church was aware that in spite of all these efforts "there usually remains in the spirit a certain hidden satisfaction and an esteem both for the communication and for oneself. Consequently, without one's realizing it, an abundant spiritual pride will be bred."[24]

St. John of the Cross further described the familiar symptoms of this pride: "This is quite evident from the displeasure and aversion these individuals feel toward anyone who does not laud their spirit or value their communications, and from the affliction they experience on thinking or being told that others receive the same favors or even better ones. All this is born of hidden self-esteem and pride. And these persons are not fully aware that they are steeped in pride."[25]

This hidden form of pride can also be associated with the acts of humility we undertake. The good deeds we perform toward others and the favors that we extend to them, while having the potential to generate goodness, can unfortunately generate evil fruits in us. The reason for this potential evil is that a hidden interior self-satisfaction is present in us because of the things we are involved in. This leads us to resemble the Pharisee who, while praying in the temple, was exulting himself above other people, though attempting not to reveal his proud attitude to others. St. John of the Cross emphasized: "Such men, although they may not use the Pharisee's actual words, habitually resemble him in spirit. And some of them even become so proud that they are worse than the devil."[26]

[24] John of the Cross Ascent of Mount Carmel (Kavanaugh) 3.9.1.
[25] John of the Cross Ascent of Mount Carmel (Kavanaugh) 3.9.2.
[26] John of the Cross Ascent of Mount Carmel (trans. E. Allison Peers in The Complete Works of Saint John of the Cross vol. 1 [Westminster, MD: The Newman Press, 1949]) 3.9.2.

Worse than the devil! These powerful words of the Doctor of the Church do not indicate that we should give up trying to practice acts of humility. Rather, we should avoid connecting these acts to the hidden Pharisees. Our struggles against this pride are dear to God, and are absolutely necessary on our spiritual journey. But we should not deceive ourselves by thinking that only the 'practice of humility' will be able to free us from this demon of pride, because we are incapable of achieving such a freedom by our own efforts.

PRIDE THAT FEEDS EVEN ON CONTRITION

Spiritual pride preys on everything that it can ingest. It even feeds on making a good examination of conscience and the contrition that comes from noticing our faults. The beast of spiritual pride can grow in us catastrophically. It is possible that in the moment of facing death we may receive the grace of discovering our entire misery (the truth about ourselves). This discovery may even bring us to ease before God. It would be an illusion to think that we were finally prepared for death, and that we were now fully reconciled to our Creator. And this illusion can lead us to have hidden self-contentment in our heart, similar to that of the self-satisfied Pharisee. So, if this is the case, we might ask ourselves why we must bother with contrition at all. Quite the opposite point of view, however, is necessary. We should try, with our whole soul, to be contrite, but at the same time, value our contrition **as worthless** and insignificant.

St. John of the Cross, in his writings about the danger of a distorted self-love and a vain attitude connected to our spiritual experiences, underscored that "virtue consists . . . , in that which **has nothing to do with feeling** – namely, a great humility and contempt of oneself and of all that pertains to oneself, firmly rooted in the soul and keenly felt by it."[27]

Authentic humility cannot be sensed. A genuine practicing of humility requires that we do not rely on this act of humility and make a treasure of it. Only then is there a chance for us, that due to our act of humility, we will truly grow in it.

ATTACHMENT TO THE FRUITS OF OUR OWN STRUGGLES

To shield us from the devastating beast of spiritual pride, God can actually hide the fruits of our interior lives from us. Oh, how blessed is that person to whom our Lord discloses only his misery. Unfortunately, there are not too many people who are willing to withstand this condition; however, in the lives of the saints there were times when they were completely prevented from seeing any fruits of their own merits.

St. Thérèse of the Child Jesus recollects one of such periods in a conversation with her sister Céline:

> Up to the age of fourteen, . . . , I practiced virtue
> without experiencing its sweetness, and I

---

[27] John of the Cross *Ascent of Mount Carmel* (Peers) 3.9.3. Emphasis added by author.

gathered in none of its fruits. My soul was like a beautiful tree, whose blossoms had scarcely opened when they fell .... If God wills you also to have this experience, then offer up the sacrifice to Him: in other words, if He wills that throughout your entire life you should feel a repugnance to suffering and humiliation, if He permits all the flowers of your holy desires and good will to fall to the ground without any fruit, do not worry. At the moment of death, your soul will be laden with rich fruits which, at His Word, shall have fully ripened in the twinkling of an eye.[28]

Suppose we do know that there is a future life, but the reality of this earthly existence imposes itself on us so strongly that we live as if the reality of life after death does not exist. The thought that the fruits of our struggles will remain unseen throughout our lives, ripening only at the moment of death, may sometimes take away every natural motivation to continue to work on ourselves.

In the meantime, the old persons still alive in us feed on the perceived fruits of our struggles, not caring if the fruits are illusory. Worse yet, the old persons may attribute to ourselves the fruits of God's action in us. Having to wait until the moment of death for our problems to be resolved prevents any disguised satisfaction, coming from the realization of our struggles with our own weaknesses and the entire pleasure that we derive from this illusion.

---

[28] Sister Geneviève of the Holy Face, A Memoir of My Sister St. Thérèse, trans. The Carmelite Sisters of New York (New York, NY: P.J. Kenedy & Sons, 1959), 37.

HIDDEN PART OF THE ICEBERG

Our spiritual pride is the portion of our misery that we do not acknowledge before God, and that is not embraced by our faith and the fullness of God's forgiveness. The fragment of our misery that we see and that we acknowledge can be imagined as being the tip of an iceberg that is visible above the water. The rest of this massive structure of ice is under the water and hidden from sight. We are incapable of bringing it up to the surface into the light unless God does this for us.

Once again, this does not mean we should give up our active renunciations. God desires that we try to humble ourselves in our thoughts, that we try to bring to light what we so cleverly hide in our hearts (our hypocrisy, falsehood and phoniness). He wants us to attribute everything to Him and not to ourselves; especially that which He achieves through us. He desires that we fight against the hidden self-satisfaction and vanity that is being born over and over in us. It is worthwhile to think about ourselves as hidden Pharisees who only acknowledge our misery on the outside while inside we are inflated with pride. And because of these hidden Pharisees in us, it is important that we recognize that we are really prideful persons. We should even go as far as to say, in accordance with the words of St. John of the Cross, we are worse than the devil.

The effectiveness of these endeavors is very small. Likewise it is impossible, by the power of our own hands, to thrust the huge iceberg above the water. Our only hope is in God. If we will continue to stand before Him humbly and consistently, acknowledging the different forms of our deceptiveness, trying to think positively about others and not to see any goodness in ourselves, then one day we may witness a miracle. At the moment of death, Jesus may stoop down to our misery; then the dry tree of our soul will be covered with leaves and in one moment we will discover beautiful fruits on it – generated not by our own endeavors but through God's mercy.

A PHARISEE DISGUISED AS A TAX COLLECTOR

Illusory spiritual supports present a serious danger, precisely because they are very subtle and difficult to notice. Even the commendable practice of aspiring to imitate great saints can be linked to a hidden concentration on ourselves and seeking spiritual progress. Instead of allowing the Holy Spirit Himself to lead us and take care of our spiritual development, we try to run after the mirage.

It is so important that we clearly understand the advice our Lord Jesus Christ gave to St. Faustina Kowalska when He said that she should give over her misery to Him.[29] We should not forget that this took place during an advanced stage in her spiritual life. Perhaps, it was the stage when Jesus was expecting from her something that, in a sense, He Himself intended to realize in her life. She only needed encouragement to beg Jesus to stoop down upon her so that He Himself would offer up her misery to the Heavenly Father.

---

[29] St. Maria Faustina Kowalska, *Diary: Divine Mercy in My Soul*, 1318 (Stockbridge, MA: Marians of the Immaculate Conception, 2001), 473.

How different is the situation of a person who is very far from the holiness of St. Faustina. When we try to give over to God our misery, we surprisingly acknowledge that this misery does not vanish but **comes back** to us. It can be compared to putting some money in the collection box at church when the money seems to be glued to the person's hand. The person makes the gesture of giving the offering, but instead, puts it back into his pocket.

Giving our misery to God can be only an illusion. This illusion disappears very promptly in concrete situations of life when our misery awakens in us again. At that time, we are made aware that we truly did not give it over and that we remain as sick as before. We see that our misery strongly clings to us, just as the money seems glued to the hand. Worse yet, our misery is in fact *very strongly* rooted in us.

When we are more fully united with Jesus, it is He Himself who can actually give over our misery, which clings to us, to our Heavenly Father. But for now, when we meet with Him we can only do what we usually do when we visit a physician—we can only describe the symptoms, talk about the sickness that exists in our body, and ask for advice on how to get cured. We cannot transfer our sickness to the doctor.

A similar thing takes place between us and our Divine Physician. We bring to Him the proof of our misery; we accuse ourselves before Him and beg for His grace. When we ponder our misery, we must not forget about the certain need of a **sense of balance**. If somebody who is trying to imitate saints is humbling himself before God as zealously as St. Faustina or St. Vincent Pallotti, then he can actually fall into the dangerous trap of the illusion that he is similar to them already.

Such zeal, in the persons who are still far away from sanctity, is possible only because, in addition to seeing their misery, God grants them the following consoling graces: the gift of knowing that they are loved as sinners and the grace of gratefulness for this love. However, when we attribute these attracting graces to ourselves, what awakens in us is this deeply hidden spiritual pride. We falsely think that in our spiritual lives we have made some progress, that we are capable of acts of humility when we ponder our misery, and at the same time, we do not lose our cheerful or calm spirit.

This is an extremely dangerous illusion – for when God deprives us of these consoling graces and we are still intensely trying to ponder our misery, we can bring ourselves to the state of absolute psychological frustration. At this point we can actually fall into the trap of despair, not finding consolation in anything or anybody.

So, our tendency to produce illusions is unbelievable! When one illusion disappears, right away we produce one or more new illusions. Because of this tendency, it is more beneficial for us when we stand in truth before God – that on our own we will never be able to admit our misery. At the same time, we must not lose our trust that we are loved by God and therefore must continue to maintain our gratefulness toward Him for His love.

CHAPTER 11

SO THAT THE GRAIN CAN GRADUALLY DIE

D uring the time of purification, the soul is abandoning supports that are rooted in distorted self-love. Then, the soul gradually dies to itself and to everything that is not God. After this, what takes place is the transforming union with our Lord and Redeemer.

SPIRITUAL CRUMBS

An important scope by which God guides a human soul in the process of purification is through the realm of his prayer. If prayer is bringing us inner satisfaction and we are convinced that we are praying well, then prayer can easily become a human reliance for us. If we experience at the emotional-level a sense of being poor-in-spirit tax collectors, relying solely on our Savior, deep down we may be behaving like a wealthy man in possession of the 'secret device' for securing God's mercy. Consequently, we will rely on this 'treasure'. Only when God begins to purify us from spiritual pride and renders us truly poor (by depriving us of the emotional experiences in our prayer life that fostered reliance) are we compelled to trust God more than our feelings.

In this way our Loving Father heals us from the illusions that our spiritual lives belong to us and that we can possess them. Praying with ease is not a human merit, but a gift from God, and freely given gifts may be taken away at any time. We must not be surprised or sad if this happens. By taking away the spiritual comfort that prayer offers when it is based on emotions, God impels us to make a greater **effort in our faith**, so that we can rely on God alone.

Praying can become a difficult experience for us. We may clearly see that we are incapable of praying. The more we have been convinced of our own ability to pray, the more we feel akin to a disinherited wealthy man. One, who until that very moment had been sitting at the table with an abundance of food, now has to be content with meager leftovers. Like the Canaanite woman, we will be fed with crumbs.

Once we have achieved a certain stage of spiritual life we need to be aware that there is only one reality – we need to be fed with only the crumbs of prayer. We need to cultivate an attitude of a beggar, who puts all of his trust in God's mercy, without fearing that we will die of starvation. God generously pours spiritual crumbs on us, even if we do not notice them. There are plenty of crumbs to satisfy all of our spiritual needs. It is sufficient to stand before God as the poorest of all, gesturing as a beggar who stretches his hands to God, awaiting everything from Him.

Our Savior wants us to constantly cry out for God's mercy, even when we think that our prayer is worthless. Only God knows the true value of our prayer. Subjective feelings with regard to this matter can be just as deceiving as the illusory satisfaction of the Pharisee who believed that he was leaving the temple justified.

Fed with the meager crumbs of prayer, experiencing our helplessness, and seeing very clearly who we really are, we need to rely on this truth about our misery and await everything from our Heavenly Father. Without counting on any of our merits or on our 'spiritual capabilities', we must trust exclusively in God's endless mercy, which will be purifying us from the tendencies to lean on the gift of prayer separated from Him.

We can discover a clue regarding how we should pray in the words of St. Thérèse of the Child Jesus: *"to recognize our nothingness, to [await] everything from God."*[30] These words express that we do not possess anything except for our misery. Everything that we rely on is just an illusion if it is separated from God. As we have nothing else to rely on, we are obliged to turn to Jesus – our only Mediator and Advocate before our Heavenly Father. The Little Flower encourages us to abandon all illusory reliances during our prayer as often as possible. *Admit that you are nothing*, because these reliances only hinder us from *awaiting everything from God*.

---

[30] Thérèse of Lisieux, *Her Last Conversations*, Aug. 6, no. 8, trans. John Clarke, O.C.D. (Washington, DC: ICS Publications, 1977), 138. Emphasis added by author.

POSSESSED BY GOD

As we draw closer to God, not only does the way we pray change, but also how we approach different tests of faith. At the beginning of our spiritual road, we try by ourselves, to somehow be endowed with the virtue of humility. Our undertaking of this spiritual life helps us begin to learn how to control ourselves and so when we are met with different humiliations, we act as if we are really humble. However, what is then born in us is a hidden form of spiritual pride, and at the foundation of this pride is our illusion that we possess the ability to rid ourselves of all the symptoms of egoism.

When we begin to feel as if we truly are humble, our Lord has to interfere and rescue us from increasing our spiritual pride. At that time both our ability to be patient and our psychological aptness deteriorate. Our inner peace and joy dissipate with just a little stress or friction. When God takes away our ability to control ourselves, we end up collapsing under each test of faith. Thus, it becomes obvious to us that we are incapable of being humble.

At that time, we will finally realize our misconception of the expectation of the proportions between workings of grace and our own endeavors; we rely too much on ourselves when we strive to be humble, and insufficiently rely on God. Only openness to God's grace can help us to stop hurting others by our power or sadness.

'Being possessed by God' is something that has a blessed outcome because it helps us to see that we do not have any supernatural good in ourselves. It helps us realize that only God can save everyone (including us) from the consequences of any exposed pride. We will then acknowledge that if we fail to call out for mercy, it will take only a single moment for this beast of egoism, sleeping inside of us, to destroy everybody around us, and our evil will explode in an unlimited fashion.

Our only means of rescue then is to call out for God's mercy: *Jesus, unite Yourself to me, for I only see the evil in myself. I am not able to control myself. If You do not unite with me, I will be completely lost, sinning constantly.*

Our Lord wants to convince us that only He, when uniting with us, can be humble in us and for us.[31] By ourselves we are incapable of true humility. In this way, He wants somehow to help us to pray and to seek our reliance on Him. He is fully aware that our motives will remain egoistical since we are praying only because we see the tremendous devastation caused by our evil, which we cannot fight with our own strength. What is important is being **full** of true **determination** in seeking reliance on God, and only on Him. Such determination is only possible when certain circumstances undermine our confidence in our own strength, and render us helpless in the face of our own evil.

We should not worry, then, when our ability to do 'good' evaporates and we see that we are still far from the ideal of being a saint, something that we may aspire to. Why do we always have to convince others and ourselves that we are okay? That we are finally capable of doing something?

---

[31] The expression "for us" should be understood in the context of the words Jesus addressed to St. Margaret Mary Alacoque. St. Marguerite-Marie, *Sa vie par elle-même*, 94.

That, in spite of everything, we are good? Is it possible that by our 'goodness' we are trying to earn God's love? Is it possible that we will receive love from our Creator only in exchange for our achievements and virtues? After all, isn't it true that the only possible exchange that can take place between God and a creature is receiving His forgiveness and His mercy 'in return' for surrendering our sins and misery to Him?

This truth is also revealed in the words of St. Thérèse of the Child Jesus concerning the acknowledgment of our own nothingness and the awaiting everything from God. For us to receive and accept this truth, God has to cleanse us from the recurring 'pride of good impression about ourselves' connected to this notion of being 'perfect'.

It is precisely this pride that continues to impede God's plan of pouring out goodness onto the world. The only source of goodness is our Creator. Nevertheless, because of our pride, we turn our backs on Him. Instead of *awaiting everything* from God, we are counting on ourselves, leaning on ourselves and believing only in ourselves.

LAST PLACE

The process of spiritual purification is so painful because it consists of exposing the truth about our pride. God discloses it gradually and delicately, but with each attempt of disclosure we experience the very dramatic rebelliousness of our ego. The main reason for all of our anxiety is the **pain of our own pride**, which is protesting against the truth about ourselves. Therefore, we blame those around us or the circumstances we find ourselves in; we search for a scapegoat to bear what was revealed about ourselves. We go to all of this trouble for one purpose: to keep our ego intact.

This process of purification is described in the words of Jesus: "Whoever wishes to come after me must deny himself, take up his cross, and follow me!" (Mk 8:34). Indeed, we have to deny ourselves in order to undergo the process of purification from our pride of good impressions about ourselves. This indicates the need to take up the cross of truth about ourselves, and imitate Jesus so that we will desire to be the last—**to run for the last place here on Earth.**[32]

We cannot forget that Jesus, though being first, became the last. In this way, He has shown us how we should relate toward everything. In this way, He has shown us what the spirit of this world offers us, and He has revealed to us our attachments to our own 'perfection'. He took upon Himself our wretchedness and the sinfulness of our attachments. He waits, however, for us to come after Him so as to fully take advantage of the sacrifice that He offered for us. He expects that in order to imitate Him we will try to lose everything and everybody, which includes the prideful notions that we are good.

This race for the last place on Earth is meant to shape us into persons who will consciously and voluntarily assume

---

[32] Charles de Foucauld, in his notes from the retreat in Nazareth (November 5-15, 1897), says: "For me, to seek always the last of the last places." This confession is as an echo of a sentence which he had heard soon after his conversion during a sermon given by his spiritual director, Father Huvelin: "Jesus has so taken the last place that no one has ever been able to wrest it from him." Father Huvelin, *Sermons*, March 1887 quoted by Jean-Jacques Autier, *Charles de Foucauld*, trans. Julia Shirek Smith (San Francisco, CA Ignatius Press, 1999), 152, 105.

and admit, in the posture of the poor in spirit, that we are nothing and that we await everything from God. It is only such a person who will try to desire this one thing: that he will not live, but that Christ will live in him. In this way the grain can gradually die.

TESTS THAT OVERWHELM US

God wants us to begin choosing spiritual poverty as a specific value and gift. Respecting our free will, He expects us to consent to His uninterrupted intervention in our lives so that He can do and achieve in us whatever He wants.

Treating our ego very delicately, our Creator often puts us only on the verge of the abyss, so that we will be convinced that we are incapable of accepting total denudation. When that becomes evident to us, He lowers His expectations toward us and strips us only to a very limited degree.

Seeing our inability to accept various difficulties, our Lord lowers the intensity of our purification process. This should be a very visible sign for us that we are still opposing the working of grace in our lives. The reason for this is our lack of trust. The person who lacks trust closes the gates of his own heart and does not want to rely on God in everything.

This lack of trust becomes our drama. It is important, however, that we try to give up this 'good impression about ourselves' and rely on our Father as we truly are. It is important that we turn ourselves over to Him in this weakened state, incapable of withstanding the tests of faith that are sent upon us due to our inability to trust the greatest Love.

It is much easier for a person who is not self-absorbed to go toward holiness. Such a person, upon seeing his own evil, begs God for His mercy even though he does not know if he trusts His Creator, or if he is able to be grateful for His love. In his soul, however, there may be a certainty that God will come to rescue him.

Because of this certainty of faith, our Heavenly Father will always respond to such a call. His response may be totally different, however, from the one that our reason expects. In His omnipotence God can use any instrument, which in this case will truly become a reliable support provided by God. As the Holy Scriptures tell us, our Lord can make the stones call out (see Lk 19:40). Even more wondrous, He can allow this unthinkable miracle to happen: He may actually meet our desires.

DISDAIN TOWARD OUR ATTACHMENT TO ILLUSIONS

Those who desire to seek reliance only in God must be in contempt of their own tendencies to lean on anything that is not God. In the practical sense, it would be advisable to follow the suggestion of St. John of the Cross, who told us expressly that we must hold our own things and ourselves in strong contempt.[33] The more precious the gifts that God gives

---

[33] John of the Cross *Ascent of Mount Carmel* (Kavanaugh) 3.9.3.

us, the more strongly we ought to disdain our tendencies to lean on them as if they are God.

This means that we should especially disdain our tendency to foster good feelings about ourselves on that, which God, through His grace, achieves in us or in our closest surroundings. It is important to notice how easily this **hidden self-satisfaction** awakens in us when somebody close to us changes for the better and draws closer to God. It is ironic that we are able to attribute to ourselves even the mystery of God's action in the soul and to build out of that a little chapel for our own 'I'.

The person who disregards his own tendency to lean on God's gifts has the inclination to lean on God **directly** through faith and prayer. In order to satisfy his natural desire for security, this person calls upon our Heavenly Father, constantly seeking Him and desiring to cling to Him. Such a person keeps a proper distance toward everything that God bestows upon him. He receives each gift with gratitude and rejoices because of it, but he does not build his sense of security upon it. Such a person knows that to lean on God's gifts generates pride, which has to be opposed and challenged by God.

By ourselves we are unable to achieve disdain toward our multiple illusory reliances. We can only admit to the truth about ourselves: that we **cling to everything** upon which our mind, memory and experience can lean.

If we disregard these illusory reliances, it is a result of the special intervention of God's grace. Only through this grace are we able to see our illusory reliances for what they truly are. Otherwise, we will be glued to these illusions and pretenses forever.

We have to make every effort to welcome and embrace this grace whenever it is given to us. Many events depend on this grace in our lives. God can give us everything if we will just disregard our tendency to seek illusory reliance on what we receive.

After all, God Himself is the Truth and, in us, loves the truth.

PART FOUR

GOD THE ONLY RELIANCE

Live as though only God and yourself were in this world so that your heart may not be detained by anything human.

ST. JOHN OF THE CROSS
Maxims and Counsels

E ach person's life is a continuous dialogue with the Creator, a dialogue directed toward the truth. Regardless of whether or not we acknowledge it, the truth is that we are only creatures whose wealth is powerlessness. We are sinners whose only capital is spiritual misery. God wants us to acknowledge this truth, to place our powerlessness in front of His omnipotence, and to place our abyss of unfaithfulness in front of His unending mercy.

Do we have another solution? We do not have any reliance within ourselves. We can only grab onto the hand of our Creator, relying on His omnipotence and unceasing love, so that in us this wondrous marriage can take place, the perspective of which the Lord Himself unfolds before us. It is the encounter between our human 'nothingness' with the 'Divine Everything'. The Divine Everything desires to give Himself to us without reservations, to transform us and fill us with the happiness of God alone.

CHAPTER 12

To Discover God in Everything

E verything that God has created is permeated with His breath, His will and His action. The Creator is present in the world surrounding us – in animals, vegetation and things – through the very act of creation and through the concrete design that God has connected with every living thing. He is present, in a special way, in rational creatures, abiding in them as if in His own temple. The whole created world fulfills God's will and is permeated with His presence. The created world can become a true source of reliance for a person who is poor in spirit. The Creator's love also permeates every event, which by the design of God is meant to direct us toward Him and toward our union with Him.

ENCOUNTERING THE LOVING PRESENCE

If we look at the world through the eyes of faith, we will notice that our Creator is present in everything, and that this is the presence of Love – our only authentic reliance. St. Paul, in his discourse at the Areopagus in Athens, spoke to us about God's presence permeating the whole world: "In him we live and move and have our being" (Acts 17:28). If we truly remembered this fundamental truth of our faith, we would attempt to assume a prayerful posture in our contact with the surrounding world so that we can praise God, who permeates the whole of creation.

How can this prayerful posture be expressed? When using different objects, our Lord expects us to encounter the plans and purposes He has connected with each particular thing. When we take and hold a stick or a pencil, or when we grasp the steering wheel of a vehicle or manipulate the keyboard of a computer, we should try to use all of these instruments in accordance with the will of the One who created them.

We should be very careful not to abuse, in any way, God's presence in us and around us. All of our actions should be intertwined with our Creator's design, so that we would not use our knowledge, capabilities, or any concrete instrument against God's will.

In this way, in every moment of our lives we would be able to praise God, who is present in this world, and everything around us would be filled with His **loving Presence**. This constantly deepening awareness of His presence and action in the world would bring into our lives peace and harmony, and it would help us find reliance on Him alone.[34]

---

[34] "Everything brings us to Jesus. The flowers growing on the edge of the road do not captivate our hearts; we gaze on them, we love them, for they speak to us about Jesus, about His power, about His love, but our souls remain free." St. Thérèse of Lisieux, *General Correspondence*, vol. 2, LT 149, trans. John Clarke, (Washington, DC: ICS Publications, 1988), 826.

Jesus told us about Himself: "My food is to do the will of the one who sent me and to finish his work" (Jn 4:34). Food gives us strength and energy, and also becomes a genuine support. This confession of Christ, our Lord's unrelenting desire to seek His Father's will, is connected to everything that we can discover in a given moment and in which we place our authentic and sure reliance.

THE PRESENCE THAT DEMANDS OUR ANSWER

When we see God, when we recognize His presence in the world, we cannot remain indifferent. We have to choose: either to go and follow Him or to turn our backs on Him. Perhaps, because of our lack of faith, God hides His presence from us in our daily lives. Perhaps He deems the risk too great that, if upon seeing Him face to face, we will turn away from Him and abandon Him for good, choosing our own way forever.

Upon seeing Him in ourselves and in the world surrounding us, God wants us to try to respond to His presence. The recognition of His presence needs to affect our attitude toward objects, vegetables, plants, animals, and especially people. St. Bernard tells us very clearly that the presence of God in people has a distinct character: "it is in irrational creatures, but these have no consciousness of Him. For all rational creatures indeed have a consciousness of God by the understanding; but only the good by the affections also."[35]

---

[35] St. Bernard *Homilies on the Gospel 'Missus est'* (trans. Samuel J. Eales in *Life and Works of Saint Bernard Clairvaux* vol. 4 [London: John Hodges, 1896]) Sermon 10, Hom. 3.

If we would remember God's special presence in people, we would avoid manipulating or enslaving others out of respect for that Presence. We would also shun bowing down to them as if they were idols. Being afraid to crucify Christ, who is present in another person, we would avoid leaning on that person more than God intended for us. We would then know that any reliance on a person independent from God is absurd and offends our Creator.

The presence of God in every person can lead us to discover the full meaning of somebody else's sins. At times we are so in tune to our neighbors' sins. Perhaps this increased perceptiveness is meant to convey a message from God **to us**. Perhaps this situation invites us to start to convert, to acknowledge **our own** evil, with humility, and call upon God's mercy, with contrition.

GOD PRESENT IN DIFFERENT EVENTS

We can also witness God's presence in important and trivial events, and in events that are easy and difficult to accept. He is present, for example, in the following situations: a pencil that is breaking at this moment, the fact that on an even path we stumble and fall, our conversation with someone who gives us undivided attention, or when we are with someone who does not listen to us. We can discover God's presence in our child's sickness and in the proposition of an interesting job, in an earthquake and in fruitful fields of wheat.

Because of God's presence in each event, we should often ask ourselves: What does God intend by this? Why is He speaking to us in this way? If we will receive the grace of the proper answer, we will also be able to be more open to God's presence and to connect God's purpose to that event.

In the Old Testament, there is the beautiful story of Joseph, who was sold by his own brothers into slavery to Egypt. When Joseph found himself in Egypt, God was speaking to Pharaoh through various natural phenomena – seven productive years and seven fruitless years. Through all of these events, which the Creator planned with regard to Joseph, he was able to play an essential role for his family and his nation.

The presence of God is omnipotent in the entire history of the Israelites. His presence is in all of the events, which were meant to lead the chosen nation through difficult tests so that they could truly become God's people – belonging only to God. Their journey through the desert was filled with God's presence evident in extraordinary events: in the column of fire, in the parting of the earth to engulf those who were rebellious, in manna that came down from heaven, etc.

Our Creator is present not only in extraordinary events, but also in more hidden ways, such as when His presence is hidden behind the laws of nature. The constellations of stars we see in the sky are filled with His action; the entire cosmos is submitted to His will. God, who constantly intervenes in the world that surrounds us, is keeping the world in existence and influencing everything that takes place. A reflection of this truth can be found in Psalm 139:

> Where can I hide from your spirit?
>> From your presence where can I flee?
> If I ascend to the heavens, you are there;
>> if I lie down in Sheol, you are there too.
> If I fly with the wings of the dawn
>> and alight beyond the sea,
> Even there your hand will guide me,
>> your right hand hold me fast.
>
> (Ps 139: 7-10)

In each moment, our lives are truly sustained by God. No person can extend his life, not even for a moment. It is our Lord who decides when we die. All existing methods of healing, including medicines and surgical techniques, are permeated by the ever-present power of God. It is because of God that these methods are discovered, and He is the One who allows or disallows success and effectiveness in every particular situation. Therefore, even as we undergo treatment for an illness, and even as we take a simple painkiller, we first of all must pray that God will be so kind as to attach a special grace to that situation. Without God's grace no medicine will be effective enough.

In all situations – easy or difficult, pleasant or painful – our reliance must be on God, who is present through His will in all events. When we lean upon His will, we start to cooperate with the **grace of the moment**, through which our lives can become more harmonious, can lead us to a deeper union with the will of God and can sanctify us.

THE TEMPLE OF OUR INTERIOR

Thanks to our cooperation with grace, we can begin to discover our God, not only in the world that surrounds us, but also in our interior where the Holy Spirit comes as the *dulcis Hospes animae* – the sweet Guest of our soul. St. Thomas Aquinas wrote about this presence of God within us:

> God is in all things by His essence, power, and presence,... Above and beyond this common mode, however, there is one special mode belonging to the rational nature wherein God is said to be present as **the object known is in the knower, and the beloved in the lover**. And since the rational creature by its own operation of knowledge and love attains to God Himself, according to this special mode, **God is** said not only **to exist** in the rational creature, but also **to dwell** therein as in His own temple.[36]

It is impossible, of course, to grasp the meaning of this truth that the omnipotent Creator is **dwelling** in the soul of a human person. We can use images, however, to get a little closer to this mystery. St. Basil, describing the indwelling of this sweet Guest of the soul, compares it to iron immersed into the furnace:

> In the same way that iron in the fire does not lose its nature, but it becomes incandescent due to the intensity of the powerful flame, having its same nature, its color, its temperature, and by its

---

[36] St. Thomas Aquinas *Summa Theologica* (trans. Fathers of the English Dominican Province [London: R&T Washbourne Ltd., 1912]) pt. 1, question 43, art. 3. Emphasis added by author.

action becomes in a certain way the fire itself,
thus the powers of the soul by the fusion with the
One, who is pure sanctity, are sanctified and
divinized.[37]

DIFFERENT PROOFS OF GOD'S LOVE

Our reliance on God can be very shallow and merely
illusory when it is only a construction in our thinking,
a theoretical conviction that does not have an influence on
our daily lives. In the process of purification, God uncovers
the veil: by faith, hope and love He shows us the entire
phoniness and hypocrisy of our illusory lives. Then our
human calculations betray us, and gradually everything in
our lives becomes very unpredictable so that we can see our
enslavement as well as our lack of trust in God's loving
providence.

Upon receiving reliance from God, we still rely on
our own capabilities, talents and intelligence or on different
connections in our relationships with others. We still forget
that our hope cannot be found in the reliances that we
receive from God. Only in the Giver Himself can we find
our hope.

Another dangerous extreme we can fall into is the
trap of ignoring God's gifts in a heroic attempt 'not to rely
on anything'. We forget that our loving Father wants us to
have some reliance. He provides concrete situations in our
lives as a means of His help. To reject such reliance might

---

[37] St. Basil "*Contra Eunomium*" Lib. 3, sources Chretiennes, Oeuvre 305, Les
Editions du Cerf.

actually indicate our prideful brushing off of God's hand and 'heroic' attempts to go toward holiness by our own road – a road that somewhat bypasses God's grace.

When we experience different forms of struggles, it will be important for us to keep new proofs of God's mercy toward us before our eyes. Such proofs can be discovered in the fact that we are still alive, that we can think, that we can enjoy, that we can show concern or gratitude toward others. All goodness that we experience is a proof of God's love, a love unconditional and forgiving, that also becomes a specific source of reliance given to us by our Lord.

Through various gifts, God gives us reliance on Himself. The beauty of the world surrounding us, the goodness that we experience from others, even our own values and abilities are nothing other than different forms of His presence in our lives. Our hearts, however, are made to rest in Him, not in His gifts. Every gift is meant to lead us to the transforming union with God's love.

CHAPTER 13

A HUMAN HEART RELYING UPON GOD

In our interior lives, God becomes our reliance gradually, to the degree that our expectations are lowered with respect to other people, and to the extent that we experience the inadequacy of our own ego. Situations that strip us of attachments progressively lead us to an awareness of our littleness before God; they lead us toward surrendering the helm of our lives to God, believing that everything depends on Him.

It is a road to interior peace, harmony, and freedom. On this road, the desire to live in truth can be born within us since God indeed is Everything. Therefore, in light of this desire, we want to admit that God is Everything and live in a way that confirms the fact that we have and enjoy everything thanks to Him.

LIVE AS IF EVERYTHING DEPENDED ON GOD

Even though we are baptized and we are convinced that we are people of faith, we actually live our daily lives relying on ourselves instead of God. We quietly assume that, to a large extent, everything depends on us and on the various natural laws that govern the world. We ponder different things and we draw conclusions while completely forgetting about God. We behave as if we were gods who have the ability to create the world and to meaningfully influence all of the events around us through our own will; in effect, we build an **empire of human reliance** and we ourselves want to rule over it.

In the meantime, we have to live **as if** everything depended on us, always remembering that, in reality, everything depends on God. The words 'as if' are crucial in describing the proper relation of a Christian toward everything that he plans, does and intends.[38] If these words vanish from our consciousness, then we are left with a blurry conception of the fundamental truth that everything depends on God, who is present in our lives by various events and in the reality surrounding us. His presence, however, is only in the reality surrounding us 'now' – in this present moment. The future is always hypothetical, until God makes actual what is still tomorrow.

If we look at the world through the eyes of faith, then there is only one real thing when thinking about the

---

[38] "'Pray as if everything depended on God and work as if everything depended on you.' Attributed to St. Ignatius Loyola, cf. Joseph de Guibert, *The Jesuits: Their Spiritual Doctrine and Practice* (Chicago, IL: Loyola University Press, 1964), 148, n. 55."; *Catechism of the Catholic Church*, 2834 (1995).

future – only what God wants to connect His grace with; only what He intends to realize and fulfill according to His holy will. All the plans and intentions that absorb our attention are helpless, useless and illusory reliances if the Omnipotent Creator does not want to make them happen. Making plans in this way, as if the future depended on us, can be compared to juggling illusions, no matter how seemingly agreeable and sound our arguments and assumptions may be when thinking in human terms. If we remember that everything depends on God, then upon fulfilling our different plans and intentions we will maintain a certain necessary **distance** from these things – from these relations with illusory reliance.

The question arises: is it possible for a Christian to be free from illusory reliance? Certainly not, for we are called to live as if everything depended on us, and thus are forced to live in a circle of illusions. Nonetheless, it is important to call our illusions by their name before God and before ourselves.

The only true supports are those that God connects with His grace. All other supports, without the presence of God, become fictional, illusory and valueless. False reliances resemble an account in a bank that goes bankrupt; it does not make a difference if our bank statement shows millions of dollars in this account in light of the fact that this bank no longer exists.

BETWEEN HUMAN 'NOTHING' AND GOD'S EVERYTHING

St. John of the Cross wrote about this need to develop distance between ourselves and all illusory supports when he described the union between a soul and God:

> In order to arrive at being everything,
> Desire to be nothing.[39]

If we truly want to be united with our God, if we have to *be everything*, then it is not worthwhile to *be something in nothing* – in something that is only an illusion. And everything that surrounds us becomes a source of illusory support if God does not connect His grace with it.

St. John of the Cross wrote about a necessary condition to be fulfilled in our journey toward union with God:

> When thy mind dwells upon anything,
> Thou art ceasing to cast thyself upon the All.
> For, in order to pass from the all to the All,
> Thou hast to deny thyself wholly in all.[40]

How many times do we think about our psychological and material supports as if they were truly constant and unchanging in nature? We base our friendships, our notion of love, and our self-reliance precisely on this kind of thinking. Consequently, we incorrectly assume that we **can count on ourselves**. All the while, St. John of the Cross warns us that if we build our

---

[39] John of the Cross *Ascent of Mount Carmel* (Peers) 1.13.11.
[40] John of the Cross *Ascent of Mount Carmel* (Peers) 1.13.12.

lives, even to a small degree, on our illusory supports, then we value them and focus on them too much. We also cease to go toward Everything – God. Thus we are instructed to live as if we could find support in ourselves, without forgetting that true support can be found in God alone. Even if we were able to find the deep and certain psychological support that would enable us to think that we possessed everything that is best in this world – we would do well by heeding the admonition of St. John of the Cross who stated:

> And when you come to the possession of the all
> you must possess it without wanting anything.
> Because if you desire to have something in all
> your treasure in God is not purely your all.[41]

So, taking advantage of God's gifts, even the one that seems to constitute '*everything*' to us, we have to maintain a freedom of heart, and not desire the support that we find in it. Our God is a jealous God, and He will not share our heart with any idol. When leaning only on the Redeemer, the person who is poor in spirit will not desire to seek support in anybody or in anything except God. Such a person begs God for mercy daily and this constant pleading to God becomes the only means of his survival, as this person is confronted with the darkness of his soul, a darkness that becomes more evident and present before his eyes. It is this state of the soul that St. John of the Cross depicts in Book II of *The Dark Night of the Soul* when he uses the image of fire consuming a piece of wood. This material flame, which engulfs the piece of wood, first begins to dry out the

---

[41] John of the Cross *Ascent of Mount Carmel* (Kavanaugh) 1.13.12.

wood and "then it begins to make it black, dark and unsightly."[42]

Let us not be afraid to face the fact that we also need to be consumed by God's love in the same manner that the wood is burned and darkened by the flame. Our fear comes from our desire to remain intact pieces of wood, useful for making various objects. We are truly frightened by the prospect of losing our good self-esteem and becoming dark, like useless ashes; because of this darkness, we are afraid to be immersed in the flame of God's love.

The saints, in the process of being united to God, make the shocking discovery of their own misery. They discover that they are truly 'nothing'. One of the symptoms of our human misery is precisely the seeking of illusory support while escaping God – who is the only true reliance. The light of God's grace, which penetrates us, shows us very distinctly the various escape mechanisms we employ to be fugitives from God. It also shows us how ingrained these mechanisms are in our everyday lives and how hard it is to free ourselves from them.

If God 'engulfs' us with the discovery of our psychological weakness and our helplessness, and engulfs us in various events that reveal our inability to be humble, then it is in these ways that He is trying to encourage us to call upon His name for a deeper union with Him. When this union takes place, the wood of our soul is permeated with the flame of God's love. This process of burning up

---

[42] John of the Cross *The Dark Night of the Soul* (trans. E. Allison Peers in *The Complete Works of Saint John of the Cross* vol. 1 [Westminster, MD: The Newman Press, 1949]) 2.10.1.

increasingly exposes the darkness of the 'wood', which becomes like charcoal; making us weaker and more helpless, we are 'forced' again to call upon our Lord.

The person poor in spirit calls upon God's mercy without knowing how much alms he will receive from God.[43] He does not know whom God will use or by what means He will implement His support. Such a person only knows to await everything from God, for He is that person's only reliance.

This transforming union, to which we are called, is our meeting with God in whom our human 'nothing' no longer poses a hindrance and allows itself to be engulfed by God's Everything.

ACQUIRING THE FEAR OF GOD

Those who are fully united with God are saints. The surest support they have is fulfilling God's will, which becomes the goal and meaning of their lives. A similar thing can happen to each one of us if we seek to rely on God in every aspect of our lives. Unfortunately, we undertake the various activities that God expects from us and fall very easily into discouragement, becoming doubtful.

The most significant reasons why we lack endurance in the carrying out of God's will are because we rely on ourselves and look at the world as if God did not exist. This is the temptation of Satan, contained in the words: "You will be like gods" (Gen 3:5). He approaches us in the same

---

[43] "Man is a beggar before God." *Catechism of the Catholic Church*, 2559.

manner as our first parents, tempting us to do things according to our own will, without asking Almighty God about His plans.

If we truly believed in the omnipotence of our Lord, in the fact that He alone determines the face of the earth and the shape of our lives, then we would count and rely only on Him. We would call upon Him in every moment through our prayer and our persistent begging.

After all, everything depends on our God. Our respect and praise belong only to Him – this is what we call a **fear of God**. When this fear of God is missing in us, we give an exaggerated value and our praise and respect to less important things – the situations and circumstances that should always be secondary when confronted with the action of God. We are afraid of people and their rules, which in our thinking govern the world, instead of fearing only God, whose will is necessary for all things to happen.

Because of human regard, we become stagnant and discouraged when we are faced with difficulties, circumstances that we consider as unfriendly winds preventing us from achieving our goal. We forget that there are only two scenarios: either God wants these difficulties, for reasons that we do not have to know, or at least He allows them to happen.

Perhaps He allows these difficulties to show us how much we lack faith? Our connections toward people and the different 'rules of the game' invented by them is a form of idolatry because we are either too afraid of them, or we adore them without any reservations. In this way we disregard our

Almighty God. If our hearts properly feared God, if we sought reliance on our Lord and Creator in every situation, then a certain distance would be generated in us toward the illusory calculations of our minds, which are not enlightened by faith.

THE WISDOM OF OUR FAITH

If faith indeed was our reliance, then we would be convinced that there is no such thing as an impossible situation, and there would be no reason for us to succumb to discouragement when facing difficult circumstances. We would know that, in order to discover God's strength for endeavors within ourselves, it is sufficient for us to contritely admit to the truth that we fail to seek reliance on God's will and on His love.

St. John of the Cross mentions in his writings about faith, that faith becomes the most important means in our seeking of reliance on God and our union with Him. The Mystical Doctor points out that when the natural capacity of our mind is permeated with the presence of God and subjected to Him, then it becomes faith, which enables us to lean on this unending power and love of our Creator.

We are witnesses of our God, who comes to us so frequently and yet we often behave as if we have not seen or experienced anything. Each coming of our God, each encounter with Him, is a challenge that He places before us, we people of little faith: *Why do you doubt? It is about time you admit with contrition that you are thinking and acting as if I did not exist. Do not forget that* **I AM**.

What is the whole might and power of this world, which **cannot be** compared to God who alone can say about Himself, **I AM?**[44] And if that is the case, why do we worry and why are we discouraged? After all, if we treat **THE ONE WHO IS** as if He was helpless before the power of this world, it is not only stupid but also a great offense before God. God allowed men to crucify Him; in this way He revealed His own might, which "is made perfect in weakness" (2 Cor 12:9). This entire weakness, which we are struck by in ourselves and in the world that surrounds us, is permeated with the power of God, the power that alone can become a source of support for us. This **power wants to be revealed in the world,** even though this world seems to be completely dominated by various human connections and 'rules of the game'.

It is impossible for us to imagine that we can get rid of our 'fear of people' completely because it is inherent in our nature. But it is important that we treat our own tendency to lean on the system of human calculations with some degree of irony and distance. We have to poke fun at what we can call the 'stupidity of our lack of faith', which very successfully limits God's action. How many beautiful deeds and plans of God are abandoned because of our stupidity?

Our only rescue is to bring this 'stupidity of our lack of faith' before the feet of Jesus and beg Him to be united

---

[44] God, when asked by Moses about His identity, answers: I AM WHO AM. "He is always what He is, He is perfectly reliable, unchanging. Always present, He manifests His saving interest in His people, and is ready to help them." R.T.A. Murphy in *New Catholic Encyclopedia*, (1967), vol. 14, 1065.

with us, the people who by their own weak faith limit the great plans of God. Then He will come to us and permeate our will and thoughts. He will take into His own hands the helm of our lives. Our Creator's will depends upon our interior disposition; therefore, such prayers constitute the only chance for us to stop placing boundaries to His omnipotence.

TO GIVE OVER THE 'HELM' OF OUR OWN LIVES

During the period of purification, God speaks to us, above all, through ordinary daily events and situations in which we can no longer fall back on our old patterns, rules, schemes or attitudes when the helm of our lives securely rested in our own hands. God is turning that order upside-down and allowing the solutions, which up to this point have been correct, to become insufficient during this new period in our lives.

We know that grace builds on nature, but on top of that, we have to recognize the importance of the order of faith. Faith serves the goal of our union with God. Therefore, it leads us to the point where we do not direct our own lives, but Christ does (see Gal 2:20). God, desiring to teach us to constantly surrender to the promptings of the Holy Spirit and to be alert to His actions, has to turn the order that we are used to upside-down. In this way, we will learn not to lean too much on this order, but rather to be open to the **grace of the moment** and to allow Him to lead us by His own designs.

For those who are accustomed to planning and organizing everything by themselves, this task of 'giving over the helm' may become very difficult. Of course, if God illuminates us with the light of faith, then it will become clear to us that there is no risk involved in this surrender, because – as it was before and it is now – **we remain hidden in God's arms.**

As we relinquish control over the helm of our lives, the words of Our Lady of Guadalupe touch us very deeply, speaking louder to us than anything else. When Mary appeared in 1531 to St. Juan Diego, an Aztec Indian who had converted to Christianity, she encouraged him in the midst of his difficult situations to seek his total support in her:

Listen, put it into your heart,
my youngest and dearest son,
the thing that afflicts you, is nothing.
Do not let your countenance,
your heart be disturbed. . . .

Am I not here, I, who am your Mother?
Are you not under my shadow and protection?
Am I not the source of your joy?
Are you not in the hollow of my mantle,
in the crossing of my arms?

Do you need anything more?[45]

So, all of our struggles will remain difficult for us to bear as long as, believing in ourselves, we count on ourselves and seek human support. The arms of Mary, where we can

[45] Antonio Valeriano, "Nican Mopohua: Original Account of Guadalupe," in *A Handbook on Guadalupe*, ed. Francis Mary Kalvelage, trans. Mario Rojas Sánchez and Janet Barber (New Bedford, MA: Academy of the Immaculate, 2001), 200. Italic and hard return emphasis added.

find security and happiness, are in reality the arms of God Himself, who completely permeates the one whom the Church calls the Vessel of the Holy Spirit.

CHAPTER 14

GOD ALONE SUFFICES

A person who is poor in spirit and humble does not seek support in the world surrounding him or in himself. The vision of such a person is different and because of this he seeks reliance on something else. Spiritual poverty and humbleness of prayer allow this person to stand before God as a beggar, having nothing other than Him.[46] Such a beggar before God, devoid of illusory problems, does not seek illusory reliance. He counts only on the Kingdom of God.

In order for us to come to this kind of attitude, we have to be totally engulfed by the Divine Flame. This Divine Flame, consuming all the illusions in us, will protect us from being wounded during this process and will remove all the obstacles in the way of the transforming union. We are to seek this transforming union with the One who, by the power of His love, can fulfill all of our longings. God loves man, this handful of ashes, to such a degree that He wants to lead him into the unimaginable world of Divine happiness through this transforming union.

---

[46] *The Catechism of the Catholic Church*, 2559, calls humility as being "ready to receive freely the gift of prayer," while it defines a praying person as "'a beggar before God.'"

PRAYER OF THE BEGGAR

In the Lord's Prayer, Jesus Christ Himself left us a wonderful analysis of the appropriate spiritual posture that we should assume before God – the posture of a beggar, one without any other support than God.

Our Father, who art in heaven, hallowed be Thy name. Thy Kingdom come. Thy will be done on earth as it is in heaven – it is with these words that God's beggar prays to the Creator, to his Father, who is in heaven. Turning to Him in this way, he wants to honor the greatness of the Almighty Creator and ask Him for that which is most important for the beggar's existence. The demands of the beggar determine his relationship to God and the hierarchy of importance of the problems in his life.

When we honor God's name, when we give Him due praise and glory, and every knee bends at the sound of His Name – isn't that the immersion in the spirit of heaven? Isn't the calling upon the coming of the Kingdom of God also a begging for heaven to come upon us now? Isn't this what God's beggar is yearning and sighing for? The road to this goal is the fulfilling of God's will. *Thy will be done, on earth as it is in heaven –* this is what is important for the beggar of God and so he demands it; he begs for it.

We then see in the Lord's Prayer numerous goods that this beggar of God should ask for secondarily. *Give us this day our daily bread –* these words show us that we have the right to beg for everything necessary for a worthy life, but it has to be placed in the context of God's will.

140

Just as bread is the food and nourishment for the body, forgiveness of sins is necessary for the soul of God's beggar. This is why he asks immediately after begging for bread: *And forgive us our trespasses, as we forgive those who trespass against us.* This need is most important from the point of view of eternal life – without forgiveness of transgressions, there can be no salvation. The essence of this prayer is not merely a plea for forgiveness. God's beggar in this situation is putting his egoism into check. It is as if he is putting a rope around his neck, as if he is saying: if I will not be merciful to those who offend me, nothing will be forgiven me.

God's beggar is a person who is aware that without God's support he will fall. Knowing this, he pleads: *And lead us not into temptation, but deliver us from evil.* This petition also contains this thought: gifted with free will, a sinner does not have to be tempted in order to fall. Even if God shields us from temptations we still are able to sin. Therefore, God's beggar asks: *deliver us from evil,* which means, do not allow evil to happen.

THE POSTURE OF GOD'S BEGGAR

Further analysis of the Lord's Prayer shows us very clearly what kind of attitude God's beggar has to assume toward the world, so as to avoid illusory supports. We have to ask ourselves this question: Is the hierarchy that is portrayed in the Lord's Prayer reflected in our way of life? Perhaps we will discover that this hierarchy is not portrayed in our way of life.

All of **our pretenses** are **contradictory to** the posture of a beggar. Naturally, a person supported by somebody else's alms does not make any conditions, such as: "I am only accepting bills higher than $50." That person would not receive anything if he made such demands. A beggar accepts with gratitude every offering given to him and is free from the posture of pretenses.

It is very typical for a beggar to have the conviction that, in reality, the gesture of reaching out his open hands for alms is worth doing. For some, the things that they receive become their only means of support. If it were impossible for them to survive by this method, they would probably change their way of supporting themselves. Therefore, if you do not want to live in illusion and when you desire to be freed from illusions, then admitting that you are God's beggar, you should be convinced that He would not refuse you His alms. Standing before God with your hands outstretched in this gesture of begging, you will always receive what is precious to you. If you are not anticipating this, then you are not living in truth or seeking your support in God.

The beggar is such only when he is begging. When he stops begging, he very quickly begins to think that he is somebody else. Perhaps he put away some money he had received. The moment he stops begging and dresses up nicely, people will no longer think to call him a beggar. Speaking in the spiritual sense, it does not matter whether you stop begging because you are preoccupied with your current work, or whether it happens while kneeling at prayer; the moment you stop turning to God with the humble plea for mercy, you immediately cease to acknowledge the truth that you will always remain as a beggar before God.

If you realize, however, that you are not a true beggar before God, then you must entrust this newly discovered misery to your Redeemer. Ask Him. Beg Him to come to you and to unite Himself with you. Then, as a true beggar, you might discover God in everything that surrounds you: in objects, events, endeavors, people, and so forth.

LIKE THE BLIND BEGGAR FROM JERICHO

"Without me you can do nothing" (Jn 15:6). These words signify total dependence on God in everything, similar to the dependence that exists in a little child or a man who has nothing – a beggar. Therefore, it is not about 'becoming a beggar' and thereby endearing ourselves to God. In reality, **we are beggars**. All that we have and all that we are comes as a gift from God; these are His alms to us. God is in love with truth, not with the 'assuming posture of a beggar'. He expects that we will try to acknowledge, recognize, and live with the truth about our condition of being beggars. Remaining in illusion is always damaging and dangerous. Why then, is it so difficult for us to admit to our true status as God's beggars?

Cardinal Joseph Ratzinger shares similar surprise when asking why we do not want to place before God our existence, "including our inability to pray and believe." He sees the main cause of our repressions and even the neuroses of the contemporary person in the attachment to false self-reliance. "A person is a beggar of God," said St. Augustine and Cardinal Ratzinger adds that "we should never feel proud, but in humility confess our true human condition before God, our state of helplessness, our need to be able to call, to be allowed to speak, and to have the confidence to beg."[47]

God's beggar, living in truth, knows very well that on his own he truly **has nothing**. He also knows that it is impossible to live by nothing and lean on nothing. And because of this, his entire existence becomes unceasing, eager calling upon God as the only real and true reliance. St. Teresa of Avila said, "What we must do is beg like the needy poor before a rich and great emperor, and then lower our eyes and wait with humility."[48]

Cardinal Ratzinger reminds us that when we say the words "*Kyrie eleison*" (Lord have Mercy) during the Holy Mass we are re-living the situation near Jericho, when the blind beggar called upon God (see Mk 10:46-52). With this plea "we admit of who we truly are and who He is for us." He also points out that because we attest to the truth, "we say: Look on me God, I am nothingness, but You are everything; I am poor and in need, but You are all immeasurably rich and able to heal all the needs of the world. I am sinful and evil, but You are full of lavish love."[49]

[47] Josef Ratzinger, *Mitarbeiter der Wahrheit: Gedanken für jeden Tag*, 17, 3 (Munich: 1979).
[48] Teresa of Avila *The Interior Castle, The Fourth Dwelling Places* vol. 2 (trans. Kieran Kavanaugh and Otilio Rodriguez in *The Collected Works of St. Teresa of Avila* [Washington DC: ICS Publications, 1987]) 3.5.
[49] Josef Ratzinger, *Mitarbeiter der Wahrheit: Gedanken für jeden Tag*, 17, 3.

THE INCREASING DARKNESS

In answer to the call of God's beggar, our Lord comes to be united with him. St. John of the Cross portrays this process of being united with God as the image of a piece of wood that is burnt away in the flame of God's love.[50]

This process of being consumed in the flames of God's love reveals **the darkness** of the soul; it shows the truth about us and leads us to lose the reliance on ourselves. How can we believe in something that is total darkness? How can we seek reliance on that? This darkness is like burnt wood, like black ashes - it can give light and warmth only when it is immersed in the flame. By itself, it can never give support; only the flame, engulfing this darkness, can be the support. Gradually, all of our illusions are consumed by God's love. Consequently, this darkness of our soul, which is constantly being discovered, becomes the 'necessary companion' of our experiences on our road to holiness.

We do not have to be afraid when our condition worsens. At a certain point we can even say, "so much the

---

[50] St. John of the Cross wrote about "purgative and loving knowledge, or Divine light" which prepares the soul "for perfect union with it in the same way as fire acts upon a log of wood in order to transform it into itself; for material fire, acting upon wood, first of all begins to dry it, by driving out its moisture and causing it to shed the water which it contains within itself. Then it begins to make it black, dark and unsightly, and even to give forth a bad odour, and, as it dries it little by little, it brings out and drives away all the dark and unsightly accidents which are contrary to the nature of fire. And, finally, it begins to kindle it externally and give it heat, and at last transforms it into itself and makes it as beautiful as fire. In this respect, the wood has neither passivity nor activity of its own, save for its weight, which is greater, and its substance, which is denser, than that of fire, for it has in itself the properties and activities of fire. Thus it is dry and it dries; it is hot and heats; it is bright and gives brightness; and it is much less heavy than before. All these properties and effects are caused in it by the fire." John of the Cross *The Dark Night of the Soul* (Peers) 2.10.1.

better."[51] The greater our helplessness in relation to the evil that we see in ourselves, the more frequently we have to call upon God to convert us. This situation is better for us. In the final account, what really matters is how much we are seeking our support in God alone. God engulfs us, possesses us, and through experiences and circumstances wants to gain us for Himself. God cleanses us with the fire of His love and bestows us with true happiness.

It is very important, therefore, for us to believe that Jesus truly died for us sinners; that He loved us and redeemed us as such. This spiritual darkness, which we discover in ourselves, does not present an obstacle for His love. On the contrary, when we deeply accept our sinfulness it becomes easier for us to seek support, calling upon God with contrition and begging Him for mercy.

As we discover each new symptom of the sickness of our soul, we have to bring it to Christ, our Divine Physician, who is the only one upon whom our hope rests. If we called upon Him each time to liberate and heal us, we quite possibly would not have to be sick. By His suffering on the Cross, Jesus redeemed not only the sins that we commit, but also the sins from which He prevents us.

St. Thérèse of the Child Jesus wrote about it in this way: "I know that '*he to whom less is forgiven*, LOVES *less*,' but I also know that Jesus *has forgiven me more* than St. Mary Magdalene

---

[51] A Benedictine, Fr. John Chapman, in his *Spiritual Letters*, points out the fact that the more we have disillusions and failures, the more we have to lean on God. "It is a very painful state to be in; but so much the better." John Chapman, *The Spiritual Letters of Dom John Chapman O.S.B.*, letter 26 (New York, NY: Sheed & Ward, 1935), 84.

since He forgave me *in advance* by preventing me from falling."[52]

It is important that we **always have our sin before our eyes** by undertaking acts of humility and by admitting our sin before it is actually committed. Our imitation of the Blessed Mother, the humble maiden of the Lord, should consist of precisely this. We should call upon God's mercy from the depth of our newly-recognized misery. Then God will look kindly on our lowliness and protect us from falls. In that way, the suffering of our Redeemer will be limited to the measure necessary to prevent us from sins.

THE FLAME THAT ENGULFS HUMAN ASHES WITH ITSELF

The Lord desires that we not be excessively worried about temporal affairs or the road to heaven. Our Creator wants our hearts, freed from all cares, to find support in Him alone.

St. John of the Cross, through the image of burnt wood, showed us the road to complete freedom. After wood has been completely burned what remains are only ashes; if, however, the ashes are permeated with the flames they receive the qualities of the flame – the ability to dry things, to warm things, to give light.

We have to remember that God called humans 'ashes' from the very beginning of Creation. In the Book of Genesis we see that these words are recorded, the words the

---

[52] St. Thérèse of Lisieux, *Story of a Soul*, 83.

Creator uttered to Adam after the original sin:

"For you are dirt,
and to dirt you shall return" (Gen 3:19).

Though full of dignity, created in the image of God, and redeemed by the blood of the Redeemer, a person remains only ashes, and his body turns to dirt after death. If we would acknowledge this truth that permeates the lives of saints, even in a limited way, each one of us would have a deep awareness of our nothingness. We would acknowledge that we are a handful of ashes loved by God, dirt in which the Creator of the universe wants to dwell.

Which one of us actually thinks of himself in this way? We prefer to think "I am somebody." And yet this greatness that we presume to have and with which we constantly fill our hearts, is only a mirage and illusion. All of the illusory supports that we seek in ourselves, in others, in objects, in money, and in success feed this mirage. God wants to burn all of this away in the fire of His love, because He loves this handful of dirt so much that He wants to permeate it with Himself – He, the Creator of the universe.

When the Lord gradually begins to burn away our illusions, we lose the sense of them. It becomes increasingly more difficult to rely on our own actions, even if they are connected with God's will. This difficulty arises because we are still trying to rely on illusion instead of rejoicing in truth. The truth is that we are only dirt and ashes. If we truly rely on this truth, we will frequently repeat to our God with trust: *I see that I am only dirt and ashes, and that my life takes on meaning only when Your Divine Flame of Love engulfs me. I rejoice*

*in the truth, which You have decided to reveal to me, and I beg You
to be united with me, so that Your action, Your grace, will permeate
me completely.*

If we truly want to start praying in this way, then our
'dreams about greatness' and all of the other illusions that
are attached to us will have to be burnt away. We will begin
to understand that the true meaning of our lives is found in
our union with Christ, and everything else will become dirt.

We will then see things as they really are. For
example, the gaining of knowledge makes no sense if it is not
connected with fulfilling God's will. A human brain, after
all, will become dirt, as will the majority of all the
great achievements of today. Can these, such transitory
accomplishments, destined to return to dirt, possibly be the
source of our support? Our support can be found only in
God who is hidden in every endeavor and deed that submits
to His will. Concrete activities, as well as the activities from
which we withdraw (if this is God's will), can help us to go
toward communion with Jesus, and in this way can become
a source of support for us. Similar effects can happen in
everything that we undertake as a result of God's will,
regardless of whether or not they are crowned with
visible success.

We may, for example, discover a very precious
support in the situation in which we try to help somebody,
and we see that the result is the opposite of what we intended.
We should not be surprised when this happens, for if the
Lord did not give grace to our endeavors, we could only harm
the other person. Can mere ashes, by themselves, become a

support for anyone? In reality, our ash only smears everyone who comes to us for help; even if they do not see that they are smeared with the soot of our misery. It is painful for us when we see the truth about this state. But we can find deep meaning in this realization because it can lead us to call upon Jesus unceasingly. It can lead us to constantly beg Jesus that He will want to meet with others *in us and for us*[53] because only then can we truly help them. And so, all of the events that reveal to us our helplessness, our sinfulness and our waywardness contain in themselves this chance to discover genuine support. Our true support comes only when we acknowledge before God the truth about ourselves, and when we call upon Him, begging Him to be united with us, to permeate the ashes of our soul with His flame.

A HUMAN MIRAGE FILLED WITH GOD'S FLAME

The problem of being liberated from support is equivalent to the problem of being freed from our attachments. St. John of the Cross told us that even the smallest attachment – chosen willfully and freely – is like a little cord tied to a bird preventing it from taking off from the ground. "For it comes to the same thing whether a bird be held by a slender cord or by a stout one; since, even if it be slender, the bird will be well held as though it were stout, for so long as it breaks it not and flies not away."[54]

---

[53] The expression "in us and for us" should be understood in the context of the words Jesus addressed to St. Margaret Mary Alacoque. St. Marguerite-Marie, *Sa vie par elle-même*, 94.
[54] John of the Cross *Ascent of Mount Carmel* (Peers) 1.11.4.

Like the little bird that cannot sever this cord that prevents it from flying, we too can become unable to free ourselves from our enslavement to human supports. Therefore, if the Lord Himself severs our 'awkward cord', we should be grateful for this special grace.

This purification process, by which all of our illusions are burned away, can lead us to the state where the grace of God completely permeates our soul. The process involves all of our illusions with regard to the truth of who we are and the need to stand before God in this truth – we are sinners. In the final stage of combustion, the flame permeates the log of wood completely; similarly, in the final stage of a human soul's purification, the ardor of God's love permeates it completely. For the person who is led into purification, the shedding of illusions with regard to human support undoubtedly is connected to an increased desire for God. The person finds peace only with contact with Him on the level of faith, but such contact requires a questioning of virtually everything that connects this person to this world.

Union with the Lord takes place when we stand 'naked' before Him stripped of all support, denuded of everything that we valued apart from Him. In reality, the flame of God's love becomes our only hope – if the illusions in us are not burnt away during this life, the purification process will have to take place in a much more painful way after death. In heaven there will not be any illusory support, only our participation in the inner life of God.

Our Lord wants to be united with us here on earth. He wants to deeply penetrate this human dirt so that we will become one – Flame and ashes. Thanks to this union, the Flame will engulf the ash with Itself and will give it richness and power; the Flame will share with the ash the fullness of His love and ardor. As St. John of the Cross expressed, "finally, it begins to kindle it externally and give it heat, and at last transforms it into itself and makes it as beautiful as fire."[55]

GOD ALONE SUFFICES.[56]

---

[55] John of the Cross *The Dark Night of the Soul* (Peers) 2.10.1.
[56] After the death of St. Teresa of Avila, in her breviary, a page with a poem was found. Its last words were: "God alone suffices." St. Teresa "Poesías 9" (trans. J. Cooney in *The Collected Works of St. Teresa of Avila* vol. 3 [Washington, DC: ICS Publications, 1987]) p. 386.

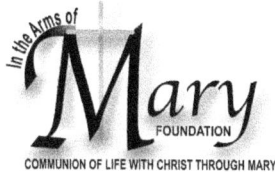

In the Arms of
Mary
FOUNDATION
COMMUNION OF LIFE WITH CHRIST THROUGH MARY

IN THE ARMS OF MARY FOUNDATION
P. O. Box 271987
Fort Collins, CO 80527-1987

If this book has helped you to appreciate God's immense love and mercy, please consider donating to **In the Arms of Mary Foundation**, a 501(c)(3) organization, to help spread this spirituality (Communion of Life with Christ through Mary) throughout the USA and the world. Send donation checks or money orders payable to **In the Arms of Mary Foundation** to the address above or donate directly on the website.

For more information about the **In the Arms of Mary Foundation** or to obtain additional books, holy cards, free downloads of *Reflections on Faith* topics, or to sign up for the Quote of the Day, please visit the website at **www.IntheArmsofMary.org**.

FAITH SHARING GUIDELINES

RECOMMENDED GUIDELINES

The "Decalogue for Faith Sharing" is recommended by the Families of Nazareth Movement USA for use with this book at small group meetings. It guides the participants in a group to share their personal reflections as a response to reading the text.

RECOMMENDED PRAYER AFTER SHARING

The prayer below is recited by an individual at the conclusion of their personal sharing. This becomes a signal to others that they may now share. It allows a person to express their thoughts completely without interruption.

PRAYER AFTER SHARING

Thank you, God, for allowing me to see the truth about my weaknesses and how it calls upon the abyss of your merciful love.

Decalogue for Faith Sharing

1. **Meetings are led by the Holy Spirit.**

2. **The purpose of the meeting is:**
   - to become aware of my weaknesses and the truth of being loved by God.
   - to respond to the desire to deepen my faith.
   - to be open to others, my brothers and sisters in the group.
   - to share different experiences of my faith and how God is present in my life.

3. **When I go to the meeting, I will pray to God for others and myself.**
   - The prayer of empty hands or that of the tax collector is recommended.

4. **I will remember that I am God's child** who has the right to trust and await miracles.

5. **As a participant in our meeting I will:**
   - serve others and not count my own merits.
   - create the atmosphere of calm, focus/concentration and openness.
   - not impose on others my ways of thinking, reacting and perceiving.
   - avoid giving advice or solving others' problems.
   - speak from my personal "I" rather than use terms such as "you, we, us, people, we should, others do this."
   - avoid discussion and criticism.

6. **By keeping what is shared in the meeting confidential,** I will preserve each participant's freedom to share openly and protect their dignity as a child of God.

7. **I will not be afraid of moments of silence,** since I or somebody else may need time to reflect. Moments of silence provide us with unique opportunities for prayer and entrustment to God.

8. **I will remember to attentively listen** to what my brother or sister is saying in order to help them in the process of sharing.

9. **When I give a witness talk or share my faith, God's grace** is not only given to me but it is being multiplied and given to others.

10. **Above all, God expects from me humility and openness.** Even one person who is humble and open to God can create an appropriate climate during a given meeting that will spread to all participants. The most important and desirable goal is not the format of the meeting, but it is to be open to God's grace and presence.

Prayer After Sharing: *Thank you, God, for allowing me to see the truth about my weaknesses and how it calls upon the abyss of your merciful love.*

Book Collection by S.C. Biela

IN THE ARMS OF MARY
(A.K.A. PRAYING SELF- ABANDONMENT TO DIVINE LOVE)

This book is the fruit of S. C. Biela's many years of deep reflections and insights regarding the Christian spiritual life. In it he explains and refers to the various stages of one's interior life and offers a pathway to deepening one's prayer. For this very reason, **In the Arms of Mary** can serve as a resource for spiritual renewal both for beginners and those who are more advanced on the path toward a "transforming union with Christ."

GOD ALONE SUFFICES

In this book S. C. Biela expounds on various ways that an individual can grow in his interior life by letting go of the illusions of this world and replacing them with total reliance on God. The author guides his reader on a path toward complete surrender of self to the God of love.

BEHOLD, I STAND AT THE DOOR AND KNOCK

"Behold, I stand at the door and knock. If anyone hears my voice and opens the door, [then] I will enter his house and dine with him, and he with me" (Rev 3:20). This book leads the reader to discover the constant loving and merciful Presence of God. God never leaves His beloved children alone. He is always at the doors of our hearts knocking, awaiting our opening of ourselves to Him. Discover the different ways God knocks, why we hesitate to open the doors of our hearts, and what treasure lies ready for us when we do open the door to our Creator.

OPEN WIDE THE DOOR TO CHRIST

In this book Biela reassures the reader that there is a specific spiritual path that leads to a time when Christ will no longer have to knock persistently on the door of our hearts because our interiors will be fully open to Him. He demonstrates how the "key" of spiritual poverty will unlock the door through our imitation and the intercession of Mary, the lowly handmaid of the Lord. Then there will no longer be two, but One, otherwise known as the transforming union described by two Doctors of the Church, St. Teresa of Avila and St. John of the Cross. When transforming union happens, we will not be able to live without the Divine Light of Love. This Light will embrace us and transform us in Itself, where we will find true life.

THE TWO PILLARS

In *The Two Pillars* S.C. Biela presents and examines two of the most fundamental aspects of interior life: contrition and gratitude. He insightfully likens contrition and gratitude to two spiritual pillars in unexpected, thought- provoking ways. Additionally, Biela reminds us of the special gift and role of the Blessed Mother as God's instrument who assists the individual in growing in the authentic contrition and gratitude necessary when following the path to sanctity.

ANOTHER BOOK IN THIS SPIRITUALITY

THE GIFT OF FAITH by Father Tadeusz Dajczer

An international bestseller in the field of Christian spirituality, this book about the interior life is a call to abandon oneself to God according to the Gospel edict: "unless you turn and become like children, you will not enter the kingdom of heaven" (Mt 18:3). With simplicity and clarity, the author manages to draw the reader's attention and awaken the yearning to experience God and follow a specific path toward sanctity.

PRAYER CARD

Listen. Put it into your heart,

my smallest child,

that the thing that frightened you,

the thing that afflicted you is nothing:

Do not let it disturb you...

Am I not here, I who am your mother?

Are you not under my shadow

and protection?

Am I not the source of your joy?

Are you not in the hollow

of my mantle,

in the crossing of my arms?

Do you need something more?

Words of Our Lady of Guadalupe
Mother of the Americas
to St. Juan Diego, December, A.D. 1531

In the Arms of **Mary** FOUNDATION
COMMUNION OF LIFE WITH CHRIST THROUGH MARY

www.InTheArmsofMary.org
1-800-451-1321

Obtain 3 x 5 inch colored cards
at www.IntheArmsofMary.org.

www.ingramcontent.com/pod-product-compliance
Lightning Source LLC
Chambersburg PA
CBHW022023090426
42739CB00006BA/261